Judicial Decision Making in Ci

Judicial Decision Making in Civil Law

Determinants, Dynamics, and Delusions

Raimond W.M. Giard (ed.)

eleven
international publishing

Published, sold and distributed by Eleven International Publishing
P.O. Box 85576
2508 CG The Hague
The Netherlands
Tel.: +31 70 33 070 33
Fax: +31 70 33 070 30
e-mail: sales@budh.nl
www.elevenpub.com

Sold and distributed in USA and Canada
International Specialized Book Services
920 NE 58th Avenue, Suite 300
Portland, OR 97213-3786, USA
Tel: 1-800-944-6190 (toll-free)
Fax: +1 503 280-8832
orders@isbs.com
www.isbs.com

Eleven International Publishing is an imprint of Boom uitgevers Den Haag.

Cover photograph: *Painting of Dazzle-ships in Drydock at Liverpool* by Edward Wadsworth (1919).
ISBN 978-94-90947-49-1

Printed in The Netherlands

Preface

All legal professionals are problem-solvers and therefore constantly in the business of analysis, normative judgment and decision making. When ruling a case, the core foundational factors for judges are legality, rationality, impartiality and the justification requirement of their decisions. However, at the same time, they are constantly confronted with the problem of uncertainty and the risk of error or ignorance in fact-finding. So in the process of determining rights, duties, or liabilities judges need to account for the possibility of error.

The legal system is a fundamentally complex system and such systems are intrinsically risky. Given the public importance of the legal organisation and the consequences of miscarriages of judgment we ardently wish to reduce the chance of error, but the processes involved are intrinsically, and to a degree, irreducibly precarious. Catastrophe is always just around the corner.

From this it is evident that human operators have dual roles: not only as producers but also as defenders against failure. The second function requires that we gain insights when, how, and why we may err. We first need a detailed cartography of pitfalls, followed by an indepth analysis of their occurrence. Only then we can start to think of therapeutical measures. Many of these insights on how we may err come from social and cognitive psychology.

Since the law is a normative endeavour, we not only ask for descriptive but also for prescriptive conclusions from the aforementioned psychological research. This implies not only asking how do judges decide but also trying to find an appropriate answer to how they should decide?. A central theme is the observation that the most significant psychological difference between individuals who were involved in events leading up to a mishap and those who are called upon to investigate it after it has occurred, is knowledge of the outcome, so there is a real risk of outcome bias. What corrective procedures will we need?

This book contains a collection of papers confronting these issues from a seminar on determinants, dynamics and delusions of judicial decision making which was held on the occasion of the inaugural lecture of Jeffrey J. Rachlinski, accepting the *Erasmus Chair of Empirical Legal Studies* at Erasmus School of Law Rotterdam, the Netherlands.

Table of Contents

1 Judicial Decision Making: The Truth, the Whole Truth and Nothing but the Truth?

Raimond W.M. Giard

1.1 Introduction

One of the cornerstones of a civil society is that its legal system makes fair and accurate decisions concerning guilt and innocence.[1] Jurists – and judges in particular – are consequently in the business of judgment and decision making. The essence of their work is the combination of the investigative and the normative. The legal core business obviously is the pursuit of truth. But what is this elusive thing called 'truth'? How do we find it? Where do we find it? How do we recognize it? Can we find it anyway? And is it genuinely the principle aim of legal judgment?

The German philosopher Friedrich Nietzsche (1844-1900) shattered the foundational idea of an absolute truth: 'There is no truth, there are only interpretations'. So, in his view, 'truth' has more to do with perspective. From varying positions, the world may look different; consequently there may be more than just one 'truth'. For the sufferer of a medical mishap the truth will be the supposed neglectful conduct of the attending physician, the psychology of blame.[2] For the doctor involved in the unhappy upshot it will be a complication from the intervention, it is definitely not his or her personal fault. A medical expert asked to look into this misfortune may recognize a familiar pattern and focus on the situational context as a major cause. At least three different views are given on the same event. But does this plurality of possibilities preclude the existence of any higher-order truth underlying the different perceptions? Are we observing a gloomy philosophical interpretation of social and cognitive psychological phenomena? And what are the implications of these insights for the legal practice? Does this suggest that we should give up any stone-hard conception of truth – and perhaps even the realization of legal justice? But how then can we defend legal rulings if catching an unambiguous reality may be so elusive? This tricky situation wherein

1 S. Porter & L. ten Brinke, 'Dangerous decisions: a theoretical framework for understanding how judges assess credibility in the courtroom', *Legal and Criminal Psychology* 2009, Vol. 14, pp. 119-134.

2 M.D. Alicke, 'Culpable control and the psychology of blame', *Psychological Bulletin* 2000, Vol. 126, pp. 556-574.

the law is operating is the subject of this chapter. How do we undertake research in human judgment? Do we have standards for evaluating legal judgment?

To answer these questions, I will first explore the goals of a legal procedure and accentuate the necessity of quality control. We then direct at the assessment of judgment and decision making (JDM) and home in on the problems of verification of judgments. To understand why JDM may go wrong, we need insights from cognitive and social psychology and will also survey the intriguing workings of the human mind, this valuable instrument used for JDM. I will finish with a plea for more methodology deduced from of these observations.

1.2 Is the Quest for Truth the Primary Goal of a Legal Procedure?

Legislation and the administration of justice have a very long tradition, one of the oldest examples being the codex Hammurabi dating from 1750 BC. It is obvious that the core business of the legal system is to resolve disputes. In civil law, judgment is required when people disagree with each other or when they were harmed by someone's negligent act. With this private law trial the decision maker may want to bring about corrective justice, to compensate when designated, to deter wrongdoing and to vindicate.[3] To bring about correct dispute settlement, abstract principles like objectivity, fairness, timeliness, equality of arms, etc. have to be obeyed. But to realise each of those rather abstract goals, we must give them a practical swing. The explanation of a contract differs from how to establish fault and causation in a tort case but in both situations the practice must be firmly grounded in a scientific method. But what is the heart of this basis? Here we meet the divide between traditionalist and contextualists.

From a philosophical perspective, as we have just seen, a zealous quest for absolute truth might be somewhat problematic.[4] For the resolution of a dispute, the legal decision makers are forced to be practical and establish the factual truth of the case in their traditional manner and use these findings for their judgment – in spite of these philosophical and psychological imperfections. In this epistemologically uncomfortable situation we can, however, pursue two different options to reach our goals.

The first one is to shrug one's shoulders and calmly continue to work in the way one has always done before and pursue the truth whatever it may be and knowing what to do to fulfil that aim. This is legal perseverance in its purest form: this is the

3 T. Relis, '"It's not about the money!": a theory on misconceptions of plaintiffs' litigation aims', *University of Pittsburgh Law Review* 2007, Vol. 68, pp. 701-746.

4 P. Lipton, 'The truth about science', *Phil. Trans. Soc. B.* 2005, Vol. 360, pp. 1259-1269.

custom – period; this is the traditionalists view. To quote the English legal scholar Stanley Fish:[5]

> 'The law wishes to have a formal existence. That means, first of all, that the law does not wish to be absorbed by, or declared subordinate to, some other – non-legal – structure of concern; the law wishes, in a word, to be distinct, not something else. And second, the law wishes in its distinctness to be perspicuous; that is, it desires that the components of its autonomous existence be selfdeclaring and not be in need of piecing-out by some supplementary discourse; for, were it necessary for the law to have recourse to a supplementary discourse at crucial points, that discourse would be in the business of specifying what the law is, and, consequently, its autonomy would have been compromised indirectly.'

We are observing the continuing and often problematic confrontation between the law and non-legal disciplines.[6] In his opinion on *Daubert*,[7] justice Blackmun states that: 'Yet there are important differences between the quest for truth in the courtroom and the quest for truth in the laboratory. Scientific conclusions are subject to perpetual revision. Law, on the other hand, must resolve disputes finally and quickly.' In this view of legal practice, if the law wishes to be distinct, the only thing needed is a thorough understanding and application of the law.

The other direction however is quite antipodal. A wider perspective, incorporating other disciplines, is needed – the contextualists view. Knowing that we often have little means of identifying an absolute truth and hence may fail in the end, we still can spot the many opportunities along the way for empirical excellence on the one hand and recognize blind allies on the other. In essence it is choosing the Popperian perspective: is this policy falsifiable? Accordingly we are obliged to reorganise our procedures to minimize misdemeanours. This means we must critically reflect on the way we work, draw other disciplines into this matter and subsequently formulate what we definitely should or shouldn't do. Sturdy scientific scepticism – but not negativism – is the lead. The Oslo line-up in criminal investigation to objectively identify a possible suspect among several people has emerged from this approach. The same principle of blinding holds for the examination of bullets or human hairs.[8] In medical

5 S. Fish. 'The law wishes to have a formal existence', *in:* A. Norrie (red.), *Closure or critique: new directions in legal theory*, Edinburgh: Edinburgh University Press 1993, pp. 157-174.

6 *See* S. Haack, 'Irreconcilable differences? The troubled marriage of science and law', *Law and Contemporary Problems* 2009, pp. 1-23.

7 *Daubert v. Merrell Dow Pharms*, 509 US 579.

8 L.S. Miller, 'Procedural bias in forensic science examinations of human hair', *Law and Human Behaviour* 1987 Vol. 11(2), pp. 157-163.

negligence this procedure of blinding is valuable when re-examination of microscopic slides or radiographs is necessary.[9] Sketching the principles and practice of how an expert witness should contribute to a procedure is another important theme.[10]

By avoiding as many misdemeanours as possible on the one side and scientifically testing our methods on the other, we hope to come as close to the elusive truth as we can without definitely knowing whether we have finally found it. This probing approach presupposes that better alternatives to the customary style must be available. We practice rethinking and re-engineering of the phases of fact-finding, legal judgment and decision making but as legal scholars our work should be guided by scientific evidence-based principles.

When observing clashes between traditionalists and contextualists one may wonder whether this is really about how to establish the truth or merely a desperate defence of historically determined boundaries. Converting to contextualism does not mean abandoning the achievements of legal scholarship. On the contrary: it means to practically improve the core business of dispute resolution. This is the perspective of quality control.

1.3 QUALITY CONTROL

In 1935, the legal scholar Felix Cohen wrote: 'Fundamentally there are only two significant questions in the field of law. One is, "How do courts actually decide cases of a given kind?" The other is, "How ought they to decide cases of a given kind?"'[11] It is linking the descriptive to the normative. There is work to be done if there clearly exists a discrepancy between the actual and the ideal. But for that, we must first have techniques to investigate and evaluate legal practices. Next we must choose for the systematic study of how to find and implement the best methods within the legal discipline. We thus enter the realm of methodology. Finally, we must assess whether we have realized improvements. We can structure our inquiries using the following scheme, showing the three consecutive steps of a trial:

9 R.W.M. Giard, 'When is the practice of pathology malpractice?', *J Clin Pathol.* 2010, Vol. 63(11), pp. 957-961.

10 J. Sanders, 'Science, law, and the expert witness', *Law and Contemporary Problems* 2009, Vol. 72, pp. 62-90.

11 F.S. Cohen, 'Transcendental nonsense and the functional approach', *Columbia Law Review* 1935, Vol. 35, pp. 809 *et seq.*

A trial is not a random event, but it starts with a perceived problem that turned out into a conflict for which parties are not able to find a solution so it is now presented to a court. This problematical starting point is important because the way a difficulty is represented affects its solution.[12]

To probe and, when indicated, improve legal decision making we must scrutinize these blocks one by one. The first step is to investigate the possible sources of motivated bias by the claimant. The next step is to assess the working procedures needed for solving this problem: what to do, how to do it, etc. Finally, we want to judge the accuracy of the legal decision was made.

From the perspective of quality control we can see that we need insight – not hindsight. For this we must rely on other disciplines than the law, especially we will have to draw from cognitive and social psychology.[13] But looking at all three blocks integrally will be a massive venture. Could we not be more pragmatic and start with an assessment of the decision outcomes? If they turn out to be faultless, we could assume that the way trials are handled is of a sufficient quality and save us a lot of effort.

1.4 ASSESSMENT OF HUMAN JUDGMENT AND DECISION MAKING (JDM)

How do we test claims for truth? We may opt for a down-to-earth constructivist view, which states that humans create knowledge and meaning from an interaction between their experiences and their ideas.[14] But there are other ways. In his book *Beyond Rationality: the search for wisdom in a troubled time* Kenneth Hammond[15] states that we will have to use two classes of criteria for the assessment of JDM: correspondence and coherence as notions of truth. These two are perhaps the most favoured conceptions of truth in contemporary philosophy.[16] I will gratefully use this twosome for further analysis for the truth assessment problem.

12 *See* J.E. Pretz, A.J. Naples & R.J. Sternberg, 'Recognizing, defining, and representing problems', *in:* J.E. Davidson & R.J. Sternberg (eds.), *The psychology of problem solving*, Cambridge: Cambridge University Press 2003, p. 9.

13 *See* R.J. Winter & E. Greene, 'Juror decision-making', *in:* F. Durso (ed.), *Handbook of Applied Cognition*, John Wiley & Sons 2007, chapter 28.

14 S. Delacroix, 'Legal Norms and Normativity: An Essay in Genealogy', Oxford: Hart Publishing 2006.

15 K.R. Hammond, *Beyond Rationality: the search for wisdom in a troubled time*, Oxford: Oxford University Press 2007.

16 N.V. Dawson & F. Gregory, 'Correspondence and coherence in science: a brief historical perspective', *Judgment and Decision Making* 2009, Vol. 4, No. 2, pp. 126-133.

1.4.1 Truth as Correspondence

In an earlier work Hammond defines correspondence research as follows:[17] 'Correspondence theory focuses on the empirical accuracy of judgments, irrespective of whether the cognitive activity of the judge can be justified or even described.' Those who are party in a legal trial will probably expect or at least hope that the legal decision maker will rationally make a well-informed and balanced verdict that is a representation of the true state of the world. However, since it is all too human to err and judges are definitely made of flesh and blood, legal decision makers may also go wrong as many miscarriages of justice have already shown us. But how testable is the accuracy of a trial outcome? Thinking about quality implies that we first need to carefully delineate precisely what we want and second we will need feedback information to see if we have met our goals.

Sometimes time will tell that a court decision was wrong when a suspect is arrested who confesses a crime for which somebody else was already convicted earlier, but this only happens in criminal law and is rare. In the Netherlands, a man convicted for murdering a ten-year old girl in a park proved to be innocent when a few years later someone was arrested for an unrelated felony and spontaneously confessed this horrible murder.[18] We can even more actively search for mistakes whereupon we are invited to analyse these contingencies in a table where we relate the true state of affairs, the defendant is either guilty or not, with the outcome of the legal decision, again the defendant is either guilty or not. Thus, we may construct the following fourfold table:

Table 1

	JUDGMENT: GUILTY	JUDGMENT: NOT GUILTY
Truth: no wrongdoing	Miscarriage	fair judgment
Truth: wrongdoing, fault	fair judgment	miscarriage

To create such a table in reality we will need an independent gold standard, a highly reliable criterion to establish the true state of affairs – and for every case. This provides us with the necessary feedback to evaluate the quality of preceding legal decisions. But if we want to bring about a systematic quality control of legal verdicts this theoretical ideal is hindered by a lack of such a benchmark. But an independent yardstick, one that is not influenced by the preceding procedure, simply does not exist. Apart from the incidental revelation of a miscarriage there is no system for structural

17 K.R. Hammond, *Human judgment and social policy: Irreducible uncertainty, inevitable error, unavailable injustice*, Oxford: Oxford University Press 1996, p. 106.
18 The Schiedam park murder, Dutch Supreme Court, 25 January 2005, LJN AQ9834.

feedback, so systematic objective empirical evaluation is virtually impossible. Do we have any alternative means for probing the quality of legal decisions?

Referring the case to a higher court may challenge the first legal decision. This new procedure may indeed reveal shortcomings or even misdemeanour of the lower court, but its mode of operation is not totally independent and may be prone to the same misguiding mechanisms as in the first instance and is essentially based on the same, sometimes flawed, data. In short, it lacks true scientific objectivity. In addition, in the majority of rulings from the primary court no appeals are instituted. So this type of quality control is at best incidental, but definitely not systematic.

The odd miscarriages of justice that come to our knowledge must be the proverbial tip of the iceberg. There is good reason to question the assumption that a court's decision of guilt is 'beyond reasonable doubt' simply because it has extensively been shown that any human decision making is prone to different kinds or errors.[19] In this respect legal practice differs from medical practice.

When things go wrong in health care the attending physician is often but not always directly confronted with the consequences of an incorrect diagnosis or a wrong therapeutic intervention and is hence motivated to prevent the incident from happening again. When it occurs this feedback is swift, direct and confronting. Few judges however are troubled with their wrongdoings and should they come forth this information is late and indirect. So there is an enormous feedback asymmetry. The legal community lacks a regular response on the result of their legal projects and hence a motivating mechanism is not there; complacency may be looming.

This leaves us with a discomforting conclusion: in legal practice the correspondence criterion for truth is unavailable. How useful then is the coherence criterion?

1.4.2 Truth as Coherence

Let us again start with Hammond's definition of coherence: 'Coherence theorists have opposite interests; they examine the question of whether an individual's judgment processes meet the test of rationality-internal consistency-irrespective of whether the judgment is empirically accurate. Indeed, no test of empirical accuracy may be available in principle or fact.'[20]

19 *See* the Innocence Project: <www.innocenceproject.org>.
20 *See* reference 17, p. 106.

This approach is very much included in the discipline of law. The practice of law presupposes a coherent system of principles and rules and legal decision makers are trained to follow that mode of operation. This rule following will vouch for a good result, for procedural justice. But there is a very disquieting phrase in this declaration: '...irrespective of whether the judgment is empirically accurate.' It assumes that a correct legal procedure based on wrong facts is possible and in spite of this limitation the verdict is both valid and lawful.

So far, in our quest for yardsticks for the determination of truth, we have seen that the criteria of correspondence and coherence mean will leave us with the displeasing feeling that either we cannot use them (correspondence) or they are too abstract and consequently impracticable (coherence). This leaves us with the still unanswered question of how we can give all trial participants a crystal-clear explanation why this verdict is the best possible outcome.

In a general sense the outcome of a trial can be erroneous for two different and sometimes simultaneous reasons: either something went wrong procedurally (legal) or empirically (fact-finding and interpretation). If we feel strongly about warranting the best possible outcome, we must address possible omissions in both groups, but how? Can we borrow from other disciplines, for instance medicine? Here too, mistakes van have grave consequences, so how do they organize quality control? The Lebanese-American physician Avedis Donabedian devised a simple threesome concept: to scrutinize and improve medical practice, always look integrally at structures, processes and outcome.[21]

Transposing this range of ideas however to the domain of law is not without problems. The need to evaluate – or re-evaluate – the structure for the administration of justice in relation to its goals, is obvious and ongoing. The systematic review of outcomes, as we have shown, can be problematic. But one thing will surely deserve more attention: workprocess evaluation. Here we will especially examine the technical aspects of fact-finding, the processes of data-analysis, drawing conclusions, judgment and decision making. These are all cognitive activities of the human mind. But the conflict arises from social interactions. It is the cocktail of emotions and cognition that shape behaviour. What then can we learn from psychology?

1.5 WHY LEGAL PROFESSIONALS NEED MORE INSIGHTS FROM PSYCHOLOGY

In civil law when people are engaged in a conflict one party is blaming the other for some reason. Blame is inherently a psychological construct and for this reason

21 A. Donabedian, 'The quality of care. How can it be assessed?', *JAMA* 1988, Vol. 260, pp. 1743-1748.

the psychological processes manifested as motivational biases are central rather than peripheral to the psychology of blame.[22] The victim's perception of the situation and its subsequent presentation to the court may influence the problem definition and subsequently the way the matter is examined and judged. It is the process of attribution, which is discussed in depth by Giesen in chapter two of this book and this subject is also touched upon in chapter 3. This is the plaintiff's perspective.

But there are other parties involved: advocates, experts and legal decision makers (either professional judges or lay-judges from a jury). They have in common that they are obliged to make professional judgments but invariably this is judgment under uncertainty. In these situations the human brain may use shortcuts, heuristics, to efficiently fulfil the task or the process of JDM may be deflected by some information and thus judgments may become biased. In 1982, the famous book by Kahneman, Slovic and Tversky appeared, describing in detail this problem area of human judgment.[23] It is a catalogue of the limitations of human judgment and as such tremendously relevant for legal decision makers but it took a while before this community became really interested in this topic. Thanks to several scholars who were trained both in law and in psychology or psychologists getting deeply involved in forensics and criminal law, the legal community was gradually permeated with this new thinking.[24] In the final chapter of this book, the subject is further reviewed by Rachlinski.

But the problems of motivated and cognitive biases investigated by psychologists are not only descriptive but also normative: they may lead to new ways of gathering and interpreting information and to new processes of JDM. However, since several years there is a new development where the functions of the brain are related to structural units using functional scans of the whole brain. How does the activity of JDM work and what does it tell us?

1.6 The Intriguing Workings of the Human Mind

The apparently simple question 'how do judges decide' is strikingly difficult to answer. Every human being is constantly engaged in information gathering, judgment and decision making. To optimize our observational and reasoning capacities we

22 M.D. Alicke, 'Culpable control and the psychology of blame', *Psychological Bulletin* 2000, Vol. 126(4), pp. 556-574.

23 D. Kahneman, P. Slovic & A. Tversky, *Judgment under uncertainty: heuristics and biases*, Cambridge: Cambridge University Press 1982.

24 *E.g.*, J.J. Rachlinski, 'Heuristics and biases in the courts: ignorance or adaptation?', *Oregon Law Review* 2000, Vol. 79, pp. 61-102, C. Guthrie, 'Insights from cognitive psychology', *J. Legal Educ.* 2004, Vol. 54, pp. 42-48 and for forensic studies the many publications by Robert Rosenthal and Michael Risinger.

must better understand the workings of our perceptions and the functioning of the mind. This is all about elucidating neural structures and functions. This subject is momentarily highly en vogue and neurocognitive science produces a wealth of information but at the same time shows the complexity of this system and lays before us the long way this research still has to go.[25] While impatiently awaiting the fruits of this line of research and the potential consequences for legal practice,[26] we have to remain practical and especially concentrate on the proper performance of the tasks required in a legal setting.

The explorations of the workings of the mind have shown that this intriguing human system has a modular arrangement and consists of two main more or less sequential and interrelated compartments: perception and cognition.[27] Perception is the set of processes by which we recognize, organize, and make sense of the sensations we receive from environmental stimuli. Cognition is how people think. Perceptions come first, they will lead us but they may also mislead us and cognition follows. The perception and its concomitant representation is the world as it is, hence truthful, but the subsequent interpretations of this perception may reflect a persons expectations, wants or desires and thus may not be genuine. Expectancy can influence perception in many ways and this phenomenon.[28]

We more readily perceive entities that are familiar to us; the unknown may be missed. We may be formidable in finding unexpected things but sometimes we perceive things that do not exist and vice versa: we do not perceive what really does exist![29] People react to what they see or experience, that is how they perceive it. Different persons may have a dissimilar perception of the same reality, as already noticed. Another important phenomenon is that expectations influence perception, an observation most relevant in legal fact-finding.[30] So each of the two mind modules is one of the sides of the same coin. We must thoroughly explore these occurrences and see what their impact could be on legal judgment.

There is another duality: human behaviour in cognitive and social psychology seems to use two different systems, designated as system 1 and system 2 of the dual-pro-

---

25 OECD, *Understanding the Brain: The birth of a new learning science*, Paris: OECD Publishing 2007.

26 J.J. Knabb *et al.*, 'Neuroscience, Moral Reasoning, and the Law', *Behav. Sci. Law* 2009, Vol. 27, pp. 219-236.

27 *See* P. Quinlan & B. Dyson, *Cognitive Psychology*, Pearson Educated Ltd 2008, chapter 5 (pp. 143-184).

28 D.M. Risinger *et al.*, 'The Daubert/Kumho implications of observer effects in forensic science: hidden problems of expectation and suggestion', *California Law Review* 2002, Vol. 90/1, pp. 1-56.

29 R.J. Sternberg, *Cognitive psychology*, Wadsworth Cengage Learning 2009, pp. 75-122.

30 Risinger *et al.* (2002), pp. 3-54.

cessing accounts of reasoning, judgment and social cognition.[31] Roughly, system 1 represents the intuitive automatic response to stimuli and system 2 is the rational analytic-systematic reaction. The first system is impulsive, the second reflective. Most of our observations and reactions are automatic and it is therefore conceivable that even most thinking and deciding by legal professionals utilizes system 1. But the general view is that judicial rulings are the upshot from rationality: only after careful deliberate thinking and deciding by the legal decision maker is the verdict given. There are many reasons why we should question this rationality assumption.[32] In this dominant Dual Process theory the two systems do not completely operate independently but interact with each other.[33] If we recognize the vulnerability of the impulsive system 1 – most errors in decision making occur in this functional unit – we ascertain the necessity to use system 2 to scrutinize the upshot from system 1 and redress it when necessary.[34]

Observational and experimental research has shown extensively that during the processes of JDM this beautiful instrument may deliver incorrect answers. Therefore, it is to important to give practical instructions that promise the best possible outcome.

1.7 For Truth More Commitment to Methodology Is Mandatory

As we have illustrated above, legal decision makers consequently face a complicated and often complex task. They frequently must process large volumes of trial evidence, some of this information is contradictory in nature and it is not certain whether all required information is available. When they must assess and combine disparate, often unbalanced, sources of information, which data are relevant and why?[35] How to interpret all these findings and finally: how to adjudicate in an unbiased way? But more basic: what is the proper thing to do in relation to the goal of this enterprise?

As we start to study law and after graduation are subsequently, practically trained in legal practice, we become embedded in organizations that have a long tradition and when we start to learn the tricks of the trade we are absorbed in a culture of custom. We believe this system to be highly rational and thus reliable but it may be both very

31 J.S.B.T. Evans, 'Dual-processing accounts of reasoning, judgment, and social cognition', *Annu. Rev. Psychol.* 2008, Vol. 59, pp. 255-278.

32 E. Shafir & R.A. LeBoeuf, 'Rationality', *Annu. Rev. Psychol.* 2002, Vol. 53, pp. 491-517.

33 P. Croskerry, 'A universal model for diagnostic reasoning', *Academic Medicine* 2009, Vol. 84(8), pp. 1022-1028.

34 P. Croskerry, 'Context is everything or how could I have been that stupid?', *Healthcare Quarterly* 2009, pp. e171-e177.

35 R.J. Winter & E. Greene, 'Juror decision-making', *in*: F. Duro (ed.) *Handbook of Applied Cognition*, John Wiley & Sons 2007, chapter 28 (pp. 739-761).

revealing and rewarding to take a sceptical step back, ponder on our practices and also dare to think of possible better alternatives.

During each successive phase in the processes of problem identification, fact-finding, judgment and decision making, we must realise that for the routine we habitually use, better options may exist. But sorting out this mode of operation forces us to meticulously take stock of those different options, give them deep thoughts and empirically test and compare these alternative strategies and finally choose the best one. Turning this way we have entered the realm of methodology, the body of methods, rules, and principles to be employed by the legal professionals.

Once we have chosen this working method, it reveals that sound knowledge of the legal doctrine is no longer sufficient: we need the input of other fields of science such as psychology, sociology, epistemology. This interdisciplinary effort provides us with additional practical normative instructions for practicing the normative discipline of law. Vernon Walker, professor of law at Hofstra University, bemoans that in the legal profession surprisingly little research and effort has been devoted to developing its own science-based approach.[36]

Moreover, the disentanglement of how a judicial case should be handled requires paying attention to two different classes of problems: issues of fact and issues of law. These two belong together like a horse and carriage. The carriage must be appropriately constructed, have comfortable springs and must be well taken care of. The horse should be healthy, regularly combed and well fed and most of all good harnessing is essential! A comfortable legal journey not only requires that we properly look after both elements but also we need a competent coachman who knows the road and how to drive the horse-and-carriage-unit.

This metaphor makes it clear that the magistrate's verdict no longer rests on his positional authority, but that the process of adjucation must be deeply rooted in a properly performed transparent procedure, of which matters of fact are clearly deeply interconnected with matters of law. It is the good old procedural justice with a modern methodological twist.

In most legal studies, educating students how to reasonably and systematically deal with matters of fact is often missing or at best rudimentary.[37] But, as discussed earlier in this chapter, pitfalls when gathering and dealing with information abound.

36 V.R. Walker, 'Discovering the logic of legal reasoning', *Hofstra Law Review* 2007, Vol. 35, pp. 1687-1707.

37 W. Twining, 'Taking facts seriously – again', *J. Legal Educ.* 2005, Vol. 55, pp. 360-380.

The most critical is that we are always looking back, knowing the unwanted aftermath – we are thus prone to both hindsight and outcome bias. 'Fact-finding' is a destitute description of the process. We do not just simply gather haphazardly facts that lie disorganized around. The administration of justice requires that facts are collected in an educated goal-driven way, handled carefully and were gathered from unprejudiced observations.[38] Facts never speak for themselves but we must give them interpretation in the context of the case. Finally, we enter the phase of judgment and decision making. For the purpose of deciding the case we must practice know-why, know-what and know-how. All this not only raises the central query of epistemology, 'what is knowledge?' but upgrades it to 'what is *reliable* knowledge?'. Because that is just the thing we are looking for.

To conclude, when we as legal professionals try hard to find a causal explanation of a conflict or a mishap – or in other words: our problem-laden quest for truth, the whole truth and nothing but the truth – this task is no longer monodisciplinary but marvellously multidisciplinary. This is justified enrichment of legal scholarship.

38 A. Morton, *A guide through the theory of knowledge*, (3rd ed.) Blackwell Publishing 2003, p. 19.

2 Attribution, Legal Causation and Preventive Effects

On Causal Imputation from a Psychological Perspective and Its Possible Consequences for the Preventive Effects of Tort Law

*Ivo Giesen**

2.1 Introduction

2.1.1 Introduction: Legal Issues and Solutions from Psychology?

Tort law is built on central issues such as unlawfulness, the protective norm, causation and fault. The tortfeasor must have committed an unlawful act specifically directed at another person. Moreover, his conduct must have caused damage, for which he can be blamed (unless his liability is based on risk). Both of these latter requirements ('cause' and 'blame') are forms of *attribution*, as psychologists call it. Their assessment has always been puzzling for lawyers as there are few 'hard' criteria for their application. In the end, it is all about the court balancing the circumstances of the case at hand.

Attribution (for now: assigning causes to events, making causal connections) is a familiar and much-researched phenomenon in (cognitive) psychology. One of the things that people in general do after an event is to assign the cause of such an event, at first instance, to the acting person; people then underestimate the influence of factors outside of that person (the rest of the situation).[1] This may affect our ideas on how accidents happen and how damage is caused. And so the question arises: can psychology teach us any lessons and provide answers that can help lawyers in this respect?[2] Perhaps lawyers use certain presumptions, rightly or wrongly, leading them

* This paper is a translated and adapted version of my Dutch contribution in W.H. van Boom *et al.* (Eds.), *Gedrag en Privaatrecht*, Den Haag: Boom Juridische uitgevers 2008, pp. 181-208. I would like to thank Esther Engelhard, Laura Klaming, Fred van Raay, Willem van Boom and Albert Verheij for their critical comments on (the previous version of) this paper and Lonneke Stevens for the inspiration she provided.

1 For more details *see* para. 2.3.2.

2 The fact that (cognitive) psychology could be interesting for lawyers and what it means, has been described by me in extensive detail on earlier occasions, *see* I. Giesen, *Handle with Care!*, Den Haag: Boom Juridische uitgevers 2005, pp. 17-24. I will omit that step here.

to think that certain behavioural effects are expected to occur. The aim of this paper is therefore to examine whether attribution as a psychological phenomenon is or can be linked to, or be aligned with, the notion of legal causation (causal imputation in the legal sense, *see* para. 2.2.1), and if not, whether both concepts can be made to comply better.

Hereafter I want to discuss the extent to which private law rules on causal imputation relate to and fit in with the actual behaviour of people, given the notion of attribution. Are there any behavioural presumptions (as held by legislators and/or the courts) underlying the rules of our civil code and case law as regards legal causation? Does this image match with psychological studies on causal connections? Or, to put it differently: do legal dogmatics correspond with psychological 'rules' on attribution? And if not, what are the consequences thereof?

The underlying, more general question addressed in this paper, can, as a result, be described as: what lessons should be learnt by tort law from the results of psychological research on attribution? Do the legislator's presumptions and intended effects match reality? And if not, should we worry? My point of departure for the last question is that if tort law and the law on compensation of damage do not correspond with common 'attributive notions' of citizens seeking justice, then there could be a problem, to say the least.

2.1.2 Details on the Content and Structure of this Contribution

In this article I will focus, from the legal perspective, on the causation issue and in particular on the second step when it comes to the causation requirement, legal causation as it is usually called (see para. 2.2.1). My main focus in this respect will be Dutch law since that legal system has a rather recent civil code provision dealing with this issue, supplying us with a canon of factors deemed relevant for the decision to be made. I will also sketch the state of affairs in some other legal systems, most notably the French, German and English system.

By focussing on legal causation I will not address the aforementioned legal issue of 'blame' or 'blameworthiness', although this theme can also be dealt with from the psychological perspective of attribution theory.[3] This theme is less interesting, in my

3 Similarly to what de Hoon in M.W. de Hoon, 'Schuld in het Contractenrecht; een Exercitie naar een Verbeterde Samenhang Tussen Regels en Gedrag', *in*: W.H. van Boom, I. Giesen & A.J. Verheij (Eds.), *Gedrag en Privaatrecht*, Den Haag: Boom Juridische uitgevers 2008, pp. 129-149 has done, but then for contract law. The theme 'attribution' is thus also addressed under the heading 'fault', *see also* P.J. van Koppen, 'Krijgen wat je Verdient', *in*: P.J. van Koppen *et al.* (Eds.), *Reizen met mijn Rechter*, Deventer: Kuwer 2010, pp. 15 *et seq.*

view, as the requirement of blame only plays a limited role in today's tort law next to the distinctive requirement that there must be negligence (in short: an act which violates the rules of proper social conduct).[4] This means, obviously, that both concepts, which are considered as one and the same by psychologists, must be distinguished from each other before lawyers can use them. Theories on the imputation of the blame, which address causality as well as responsibility, will therefore not be discussed.[5]

The theme of legal causation is however particularly interesting because psychological research[6] on attribution (see para. 2.3.1) has shown that people tend to assign the cause of an event to the acting person and thus underestimate other causal factors outside of that person (*i.e.* the rest of the situation). This 'fundamental attribution error'[7] (see para. 2.3.2) appears to be of importance with respect to issues of causation in tort law. After all, this 'error' could lead to misguided ideas on the course of events and thus lead to the wrong decisions regarding liability and compensation by courts deciding a case or by parties negotiating a settlement.

On the other hand, it is also conceivable that legal causation is based on the idea that real life, psychological imputation is not really relevant; the attribution error is approved, as it were, or accepted in any case, by the legal system as the resulting outcome is also the desired outcome on normative or public policy grounds. The same line of thought might also apply to the so-called 'defensive attribution', the phenomenon that people regard someone's responsibility graver if his conduct has led to more serious consequences. This will also be incorporated hereafter (para. 2.3.3), just as the actor-observer difference and the self-serving bias (para. 2.3.4 and para. 2.3.5).[8] Preceding these observations based on cognitive psychology, I will provide a short description of the legal framework, dealing with the *condicio sine qua non* (CSQN)

4 *See* for example A.J. Verheij, *Monografieën Privaatrecht. Deel 4: Onrechtmatige Daad*, Deventer: Kluwer 2005, p. 48. *See also* A.S. Hartkamp, *C. Asser's Handleiding tot Beoefening van het Nederlands Burgerlijk recht. Deel 6: Verbintenissenrecht IV De Verbintenis uit de Wet*, Zwolle: W.E.J. Tjeenk Willink 2011 no. 107.

5 *See, e.g.*, K.G. Shaver, *The Attribution of Blame. Causality, Responsibility and Blameworthiness*, New York: Springer 1985. *See also, e.g.*, De Hoon 2008; J. Mantler *et al.*, 'Attributions for Serious Illness: Are Controllability, Responsibility, and Blame Different Constructs?', *Canadian Journal of Behavioural Science* 2003, Vol. 35, No. 2, pp. 142-152; J.M. Barendrecht, 'Verdeling van Verantwoordelijkheid als het fout gaat', *in*: W.H. van Boom, M.J. Borgers, *De Rekenende Rechter*, Den Haag: Boom Juridische uitgevers 2004, pp. 55-56, and V.P. Hans & J. Dee, 'Whiplash: Who's to Blame?', 68 *Brook. L. Rev.* 2002-2003, pp. 1093-1094.

6 *See, e.g.*, R. Vonk (Ed.), *Cognitieve Sociale Psychologie*, (2nd edn.), Utrecht: Lemma 2003, pp. 23-25 and pp. 77 *et seq.*

7 *See* for now already S. Plous, *The Psychology of Judgment and Decision Making*, New York: McGraw-Hill 1993, pp. 180 *et seq.*

8 The observations in para. 2.3 are written from the perspective of 'ordinary' people and not the civil court judge.

requirement as well as with legal causation (para. 2.2.1) and I will examine which behavioural presumptions and intended behavioural effects might be underneath those concepts (para. 2.2.2). Paragraph 2.4 will be devoted to the application of the results found in paragraph 2.3 to these legal issues: how can psychological insights be linked to such a legal issue as 'legal causation', looking at both from the perspective of a private law judge. I will list the consequences and discuss how we might be able to improve the connection between the two. Subsequently, I will specifically address the consequences of the psychological 'results' I found for the intended behavioural (preventive) effects on the legal rules regarding causation (para. 2.5). The answer as to whether and how such preventive effects can be achieved is partly negative and I will suggest explanations. This will lead to some general ideas on the (lack of) preventive effects of tort law. This contribution will be concluded in paragraph 2.6.

2.2 A Short Description of the Legal Framework

2.2.1 Causation: European Rules on CSQN and Legal Causation

If a person wants to hold someone else responsible for damage suffered, this not only requires an unlawful act but also a causal relation between that act and the damage. In basically all legal systems the assessment of the causation issue is split in two separate stages.[9] First, we look into what is called 'factual causation': is there a connection between the act and the damage in question? This concerns the issue of establishment of liability and the aforementioned *condicio sine qua non* (CSQN) test or *but for*-test. Subsequently, the question of the so-called 'legal causation' is addressed, which concerns the normative imputation of the damage to the event that caused the damage and which is used to limit the extent of causation and liability.[10]

To be more precise, factual causation is a requirement for the establishment of civil liability in all legal systems.[11] This issue of *condicio sine qua non* is dealt with by asking the question: would the damage also have occurred if the tortfeasor had not acted

9 The so-called Principles of European Law on Non-Contractual Liability arising out of Damage Caused to Another (PEL Liab. Dam), are a notable exception, *see* below and *see* C. von Bar, *Principles of European Law. Non-Contractual Liability arising out of Damage Caused to Another (PEL Liab. Dam)*, Oxford: OUP 2009, chapter 4, Art. 4:101, Comments, B, 11-12. This seems to be based on the (assumed) different position in France (and Belgium) in this respect, Von Bar 2009, Chapter 4, Art. 4:101, Notes, II, 17, but many other authors disagree, *see* the references in the notes hereafter, and G. Viney & P. Jourdain, *Traité de Droit Civil. Les Conditions de la Responsabilité*, (2e éd.) Paris: L.G.D.J. 2006, no. 351 *et seq*, especially nos. 353 and 359.

10 *See* Cees van Dam, *European Tort Law*, Oxford: OUP 2006, no. 1102, who observes in no. 1101 that neither France nor Germany nor England have a statutory provision on causation. The Dutch Civil Code (BW) does, in Art. 6:98 BW.

11 Van Dam 2006, no. 1102; W. van Gerven, J. Lever & P. Larouche, *Cases, Materials and Text on National, Supranational and International Tort Law*, Oxford: Hart Publishing 2000, p. 452.

in the way he did? If that is the case, acting correctly would not have prevented the damage, which means that the CSQN connection is not established. If that is not the case, if the answer to the question is 'no', a(nother) (lawful) act would have prevented the damage, or at least not have caused it, which means that the requirement regarding the connection between act and damage is met.[12] This CSQN issue is, first and foremost, a question of evidence: which facts can be proven?[13]

Having established causation in this manner, the second step of the causation requirement commences; it is about finding the limits of the causal connection by establishing legal causation. This (legal) imputation of (some of) the damage to the event that actually caused the damage, will have to be taken up by the courts.

Under Dutch law, this is done according to the rule set forth in Article 6:98 Dutch Civil Code (BW).[14] A general statement on the results of the assessment on the basis of this provision cannot be given beforehand, however. The (non-limitative) canon of relevant circumstances and factors must be weighed time and again by the court which tries the case. This court will then make a choice which is (to a large extent) normative by nature, involving a policy decision.[15] The major factors or elements of this assessment are the following. Practically the most influential factor is the 'nature of the damage'. If the damage is purely patrimonial, the imputation will be stricter (include fewer items of loss) than in the case of bodily injury.[16] The assessment of a specific case under Article 6:98 BW, however, also includes the 'nature of the liability'. This issue usually concerns the question whether the liability is based on fault or risk, whether one is liable for one's own acts or someone else's (vicarious liability) or whether the liability has arisen from a contractual setting or not. What also matters is that the bigger the fault leading to the event is, the more extensive the imputation can be. This implies that the 'degree of blame' is also relevant. The 'nature of the violated norm' (traffic rules and safety regulations versus a regular duty of care) may also determine the extent of the imputation. The 'foreseeability of the damage' will also play a role regarding the imputation (the more foreseeable, the more an extensive imputation can be justified) as well as the fact that the resulting damage may be less

12 On this subject for example A.S. Hartkamp & C.H. Sieburgh, *C. Asser's Handleiding tot Beoefening van het Nederlands Burgerlijk Recht. Deel 6: Verbintenissenrecht. De Verbintenis in het Algemeen, 2e Gedeelte*, (13th ed.), Deventer: Kluwer 2009, no. 51; Verheij 2005, pp. 27-28.

13 On such questions of evidence and related problems for example G. Wagner, 'Heuristics in Procedural Law', *in*: G. Gigerenzer & C. Engel, *Heuristics and the Law*, Cambridge: MIT Press 2006, pp. 281-302, pp. 281 *et seq.* and J. Schulz, 'Rules of Evidence as Heuristics: Heuristics as Rules of Evidence', *in*: Gigerenzer & Engel 2006, pp. 327 *et seq.*

14 Hartkamp *et al.* 2009, nos. 63 *et seq.*; Verheij 2005, pp. 28-29 and pp. 69 *et seq.*

15 This is a valid statement for all systems under review, *see* Van Dam 2006, no. 1102 and 1111. *See also* Van Gerven *et al.* 2000, p. 395.

16 This is a general trend in all systems under review, *see* Van Dam 2006, nos. 1102 and 1111.

or more 'remote' from the unlawful act (the event).[17] The consequences of all this is that, in the end, there is not much to say about this with certainty, if only because the factors that must be weighed may also contradict each other.

Under German and English law (and a lesser extent French law[18]), the issue of legal causation is also highly important but no statutory provision supplies the decision maker with a set of circumstances or factors to be considered.[19] Case law decides the issue, using several different legal techniques, but on the basis, mainly, of policy considerations, looking at what is fair, just and reasonable.[20] In this regard, German lawyers will analyse the protective function of the rule which imposes the duty on the tortfeasor ('scope of rule'), while English lawyers will see whether a certain cause is 'too remote' ('remoteness of damage'), which means that damage must be 'reasonable foreseeable'. Under French law one looks only for 'direct and immediate consequences' without being guided further by fixed criteria.[21]

As to the current state of affairs within European private law, the Principles of European Tort Law (PETL) distinguish between CSQN in Article 3:101 PETL and legal causation (scope of liability) in Article 3:201 PETL. As regards the latter, the article mentions some of the factors that are to be weighed (although the list is not exhaustive) in deciding the issue: the foreseeability, the nature and value of the protected interest, the basis of liability, the extent of the ordinary risks of life and the protective purpose of the violated rule. These factors are collected from and are known from the legal systems dealt with above. The Draft Common Frame of Reference is basically 'the odd one out' in Europe since its rules (as laid down in the Principles of European Law on Non-Contractual Liability arising out of Damage Caused to Another (PEL Liab. Dam)) do not make a division between establishing liability and limiting liability but use one (vague) phrase instead, *i.e.* 'to be regarded as the consequence of'.[22]

Even without any further analysis of the two forms of causation dealt with here, it will be clear that even though the first issue primarily seems to be a question of evidence (what did actually happen?), it also includes making normative decisions (*e.g.*

17 On the previous, Hartkamp *et al.* 2009, nos. 63-69, and Verheij 2005, pp. 70-72.

18 *See* above, note 9.

19 For details and cases, *see* Van Gerven *et al.* 2000, pp. 396-426; Van Dam 2006, nos. 1103 *et seq.*

20 Van Dam 2006, no. 1111; Van Gerven *et al.* 2000, p. 454 and p. 457. *See also* K. Zweigert & H. Kötz, *An Introduction to Comparative Law*, (3rd ed.), Oxford: OUP 1998, p. 602 and p. 610.

21 *See*, in general, Zweigert & Kötz 1998, pp. 602, 609 and 621. *See also* H. Kötz & G. Wagner, *Deliktsrecht*, (11th edn.), München: Verlag Franz Vahlen 2010, no. 186 and nos. 209 *et seq*; W.V.H. Rogers, *Winfield & Jolowicz on Tort*, (17th edn.), London: Sweet & Maxwell 2006, nos. 6-16 *et seq*; Viney/Jourdain 2006, no. 359.

22 *See* Art. 4:101 PEL Liab. Dam and Von Bar 2010, Chapter 4, Art. 4:101, Comments, B, nos. 11-12, and note 9 above.

on what can and cannot be proven), whereby the person making the decision may be affected by psychological influences and prejudices (bias). The second causal step is much more normative by nature (which losses will the decision maker impute to the tortfeasor?) and requires the judge to make his own very direct assessment. This is a decision which may be even more affected by all kinds of psychological pitfalls that anyone, including our judges, may come across.

2.2.2 Presumptions Regarding Conduct and Behavioural Effects?

Prior to the further discussion of some of these psychological pitfalls, it seems wise to examine if, and the extent to which, the legislator perhaps made certain assumptions on human behaviour when these rules on causality were drawn up. It is also interesting to examine whether these rules were expected to have specific behavioural effects, and if so, which ones. If, after all, this were the case, this could perhaps pave the way for the feedback (in para. 2.4) between the legal and psychological factors when dealing with causation issues. I will do so (only) for the Dutch legislation since this is the most recent (and in fact only rather explicit) codification of the legal causation requirement.

Unfortunately, the Dutch *travaux préparatoires* on this issue are not of much help. If the legislator had any presumptions or effects in mind at all, they have not been recorded. Obviously, this makes sense if one considers that this legislation and explanation have been created by private law experts. It does not mean however, that we are completely lost as it is possible to make the behavioural presumptions and intended behavioural effects of tort law *as such* our points of departure since those points of departure may also apply to the causation requirement. It is doubtful, however, whether the legislator has been willing to show his cards in this respect. And indeed, the *travaux préperatoires* are not very helpful here either.

Does this mean that the legislator had no ideas whatsoever on what could or should be achieved by tort law? It is not that serious, but this legislator has failed to record it. A generally-recognized point of departure of extra-contractual liability, however, and that is something I will assume below, is that the rules of tort law aim to find a balance between the need for safety (for the injured party) on the one hand, and the need for freedom of actions (for the addressed party) on the other. Today, the safety aspect has become more and more emphasized,[23] and this results in a broad recognition of at least two functions of tort law: the first one is the award of damages, which means that compensation must be provided if the other party acted wrongly or neg-

23 *See* for example Verheij 2005, p. 16, C.C. van Dam, *Aansprakelijkheidsrecht*, Den Haag: Boom Juridische uitgevers 2000, no. 001; Hartkamp & Sieburgh 2011, no. 12.

ligently, and secondly, whenever possible, the prevention of negligent behaviour by sanctioning such behaviour.[24]

Taking these functions of tort law as a point of reference, it is not too difficult to assume that the behavioural presumption underlying tort law in general is that the enforceable duty to pay damages in the case of negligent behaviour will lead to the actor avoiding such negligent (and as a result, unlawful) acts in future. This in turn implies that the legislator assumes and pre-supposes that negligent behaviour will be avoided due to the sanction it carries. When subsequently the actor actually displays such behaviour, damage as such is prevented and this is the intended behavioural effect, which is generally considered to be the result of tort law. The degree in which this effect occurs in reality (whether the rules of tort law really have a preventive effect) is a moot point,[25] which I will return to in paragraph 2.5.

Using all this as the point of departure, we can subsequently establish that the rules regarding causality are an important part of this bigger whole and therefore we can safely say that the same presumptions and effects will also play a role at that level. It is now time to consider whether all this fits in with the lessons of (cognitive) psychology on causal connections.

2.3 Psychological Insights

2.3.1 *Several Attribution Theories*

The part of psychology that is devoted to attribution theory, in the broadest sense of the word, 'is concerned with the attempts of ordinary people to understand the causes and implications of the events they witness'.[26] People are 'seeking to discover why an event has occurred'.[27] It is important to note that there is not just one attribution theory, but rather a number of related theories that describe how people assign

24 *See* Verheij 2005, pp. 16-17, where other less generally-recognized functions are mentioned. I will ignore these here.

25 On this in general, W.H. van Boom, 'Compensating and Preventing Damage: is there any Future Left for Tort Law?', *in*: *Festkrift till Bill W. Dufwa - Essays on Tort, Insurance, Law and Society in Honour of Bill W. Dufwa. Volume I*, Stockholm: Jure 2006, pp. 287 *et seq*., and E.F.D. Engelhard, *Regres*, Deventer: Kluwer 2003, pp. 213-222.

26 L. Ross & C.A. Anderson, 'Shortcomings in the Attribution Process: On the Origins and Maintenance of Erroneous Social Assessments', *in*: D. Kahneman *et al.* (Eds.), *Judgement under Uncertainty: Heuristics and Biases*, Cambridge University Press, Cambridge 1982 (reprint 2001), p. 129. The following is a very brief reflection of only a part of the theories on this subject.

27 B. Weiner, 'Attribution, Emotion, and Action', *in*: R.M. Sorrentino & E.T. Higgins, *Handbook of Motivation and Cognition*, New York: The Guilford Press 1986, p. 292. *See also* Van Koppen 2010, p. 17.

the causes of events or acts.[28] An event can be an accident, but also something someone said or the result of certain acts.[29] The event can be the actor's own conduct or the act of someone else.[30]

This search for answers regarding the possible causes of events or acts is something people do not always engage in because that would be too much of a (cognitive) effort. Instead, people look in particular for explanations when something unexpected happens, when a wish is not fulfilled or when the outcome is of major importance. People are said to do so in order to prevent surprises and uncertainties from happening and to (be able to) control them. By doing so, people also want to achieve certain goals next time around, they want to learn.[31]

One of the founding fathers of attribution theory, Heider, distinguished three possible causes or actually three factors as possible causes for certain events. Firstly, 'the self', which means the person who acted; secondly someone else and thirdly coincidence or 'fate'.[32] Within this theory the first factor must be distinguished from the second and third one. So 'dispositional (personal) attribution' (to assign something to the person of the actor), also called internal attribution, is juxtaposed to external or 'situational attribution' (to assign something to factors outside of the actor, either another person or the situation).[33] The next important part of the theory concerns the stability of a cause. Does it apply temporarily or permanently? A permanent or stable cause, such as someone's personal characteristics, enables us to predict behaviour. It provides something to hold on to.[34]

28 *See* for example L.A. McArthur, 'The How and What of Why?', *Journal of Personality and Social Psychology* 1972, Vol. 22, No. 2, p. 171. Attribution is in itself only a part of the human 'information-processing system', *see* D.L. Hamilton, 'Causal Attribution Viewed from an Information-processing Perspective', *in*: D. Bar-Tal & A.W. Kruglanski, *The Social Psychology of Knowledge*, Cambridge: Cambridge University Press 1988, pp. 359 *et seq.*

29 Vonk *et al.* 2003, p. 23 and p. 78.

30 *See* Vonk *et al.* 2003, p. 97 and p. 117; R.E. Nisbett *et al.*, 'Popular Induction: Information is not Necessarily Informative', *in*: D. Kahneman *et al.* (Eds.), *Judgement under Uncertainty: Heuristics and Biases*, Cambridge: Cambridge University Press 1982 (reprint 2001), p. 103.

31 *See* Weiner 1986, pp. 292-293. *See also* R. Vonk (Ed.), *Sociale Psychologie*, (2nd edn.), Groningen/Houten: Wolters-Noordhoff 2007, pp. 210-212, and in particular Vonk *et al.* 2003, p. 117: attribution occurs when someone is important, something negative happens or when someone does something unexpected.

32 Vonk *et al.* 2003, p. 23 and p. 78.

33 Vonk *et al.* 2003, p. 78; Van Koppen 2010, p. 17.

34 *See* for more details Van Koppen 2010, pp. 17-18, and Vonk *et al.* 2007, pp. 208-212. Attributing either internally or externally thus also depends, for example, on whether a good person acts correctly (consistent behaviour, internal attribution) or acts incorrectly (inconsistent; external), D.T. Regan, E. Straus & R. Fazio, 'Liking and the Attribution Process', *Journal of Experimental Social Psychology* 1974, 10, pp. 385-397.

Kelley was among those who built on Heider's work and further formalized the attribution theory.[35] Kelly distinguishes three attribution dimensions and three related sources of information. There is consistency information, which refers to the individual's behaviour at another moment or to another modality; consensus information, which refers to the behaviour of other actors[36] and distinctiveness information, which is related to the objects (entities) with respect to which the behaviour occurs.[37] Assigning something or someone as a cause depends on this information. Dispositional or personal attribution means that the cause of behaviour is within the individual, whereas an entity attribution assigns the cause to the object (which can also be an event). These forms can also be combined, but coincidence, too, can be a determining factor (situational attribution).[38]

Attribution theory thus addresses the way people process social information. It is a normative theory which says what we should do as rationally-acting human beings.[39] As stated earlier, there is no time, however, to always attribute in accordance with the theory. Sometimes we do not even want to do so. There are many occasions in which we lack information. By way of compensation we then use existing knowledge and existing rules of thumb, which are the result of our experience stored in the form of causal frameworks.[40] An example is the 'multiple sufficient causes' scheme which says that if more than one cause is likely, a single cause is sometimes already identified as an adequate explanation. The down side is, however, that distortions occur and 'errors' are made. It may result in wrongly ignoring another cause in the scheme because 'the' cause is already known; this is referred to as the 'discounting principle'.[41]

35 *See* on this subject Nisbett *et al.* 1982, p. 101, and Shaver 1985, pp. 50 *et seq*. Plous 1993, p. 174, places Kelley on an even higher pedestal regarding the development of the 'attribution theory'.

36 In the meantime, there is an increasing amount of evidence that consensus information (what do others do) exerts little or no influence on attributing causes. *See* Nisbett *et al.* 1982, pp. 102-103; Vonk *et al.* 2003, p. 133, and Plous 1993, pp. 176-178. This has probably to do with the 'false consensus effect', the presumption that any other person would act in a similar fashion as the observer in the same situation (Vonk *et al.* 2003, p. 133).

37 Vonk *et al.* 2003, pp. 88-89; Plous 1993, p. 174; Nisbett *et al.* 1982, p. 101; Van Koppen 2010, p. 18. All this is part of Kelley's co-variation model or ANOVA principle, *see also* Vonk *et al.* 2007, pp. 209-211. I will not discuss this here any further; more details on this subject are not necessary for this paper.

38 *See* Vonk *et al.* 2003, pp. 90-93; Plous 1993, pp. 174-175.

39 As said earlier, this concerns a collection of theories. I will leave untouched topics such as the performance attribution theory by Weiner, *see* for example Weiner 1986 and Vonk *et al.* 2003, pp. 97 *et seq*., and the self-observation theory of Bem (*see* Vonk *et al.* 2003, pp. 107 *et seq*.).

40 Vonk *et al.* 2003, pp. 94-95. *See* on this also Van Koppen 2010, pp. 15-17.

41 Vonk *et al.* 2003, p. 95; Ross & Anderson 1982, p. 132.

This is one of the many examples of what we call 'attribution errors'. They may have huge consequences.[42] Below I will address some of these distortions (always from the perspective of a regular person, and not yet from the perspective of, for example, a judge) in more detail.

2.3.2 *The Fundamental Attribution Error*

The fundamental attribution error is a distortion related to another (also psychological) phenomenon: salience. Salience is the ability to draw attention; the more salient factors, the factors which draw more attention, are typically considered to be the more likely cause. Hence someone's perception of causality also depends on what has captured his attention in a certain context and in which direction his attention is drawn is then determined by the salient character of a factor (or a person).[43]

If that is our starting point and we then make the link with a social environment where behaviour, and thus the actor, captures most of the attention of an observer, it is only a small step to realize that this focus on the actor will lead to an attribution by the observer of the behaviour which overestimates dispositional factors and personal characteristics, such as possibilities and motives (internal attribution), and underestimates situational factors (external attribution). This means that we tend to assign the cause of an event, in first instance, to the acting person and we underestimate the effects of factors outside that person (the rest of the situation).[44] As this tendency appears to be huge, and the attribution often mistaken, this has been qualified as 'the fundamental attribution error' instead of a regular bias. Follow-up studies have confirmed this error (also called: correspondence bias) time and again; even when the test subjects are given a more detailed explanation, they focus on the personal characteristics to predict behaviour. The result is that the same error is made.[45] This

42 Van Koppen 2010, p. 19.

43 Plous 1993, pp. 178-180, who refers to people such as S.E. Taylor & S.T. Fiske, 'Points of View and Perceptions of Causality', *Journal of Personality and Social Psychology* 1975, Vol. 32, No. 3, pp. 439-445 and Ross & Anderson 1982, pp. 138-139. *See* N.R. Feigenson, 'The Rhetoric of Torts: How Advocates Help Jurors Think About Casuation, Reasonableness, and Responsibility', *Hastings L.J.*, Vol. 47 1995-1996, p. 128. On 'attention' also Vonk *et al.* 2003, pp. 135-136, and Giesen 2005, pp. 65-67.

44 Plous 1993, p. 180; Van Koppen 2010, pp. 19-20; Vonk *et al.* 2003, p. 124; Ross & Anderson 1982, p. 135. *See also* Feigenson 1995, pp. 126 *et seq.*; W. Farnsworth, *The Legal Analyst. A Toolkit for Thinking about the Law*, Chicago: The University of Chicago Press 2007, p. 242, and R. Giard, 'Na de Calamiteit: Perceptie en Primaire Psychologische Reacties en hun Betekenis voor het Aansprakelijkheidsrecht', *Letsel & Schade* 2010, no. 2, p. 10. Perhaps this also provides a (partial) explanation for the tendency to think in terms of primary (the main responsible) and secondary actors in cases of failing supervision (more on this I. Giesen, *Toezicht en Aansprakelijkheid*, Deventer: Kluwer 2005, particularly pp. 37-40).

45 *See* Plous 1993, pp. 180-181; Vonk *et al.* 2003, p. 124, and Van Koppen 2010, p. 19. *See also* Ph.E. Tetlock, 'Accountability: A Social Check on the Fundamental Attribution Error', *Social*

does not mean, though, that the argument has never been made that this error does not exist or at least that it is not fundamental.[46]

The reason why correspondence bias occurs is because it is difficult to make an attribution that does justice to the influence of the situation. We must 'know' in which situation the actor is in, we must have 'expectations' about the behaviour of other people in such cases; we must 'identify' behaviour and perhaps 'correct' that behaviour after a comparison with what others would do. Things may go wrong in all of these fields. And when they go wrong, they go badly wrong. Take a closer look at the third step, for example: even when we know the situation and our expectations are correct, our judgment may still be off. Our perception of the behaviour we expect may be much stronger than it is in reality. Because of this we think this response is perhaps 'too much'; we conceive it as exaggerated. So even when we have a sound grasp of the situation distortions, extreme conclusions still occur.[47]

2.3.3 Defensive Attribution

The next feature related to attribution theory is what is termed defensive attribution; the phenomenon that people assign more responsibility to other individuals (the actor or the victim) if the conduct has more serious consequences.[48] This is a defensive distortion because people guard themselves against the unbearable thought that negative events with serious consequences happen accidentally, which means it can happen to you, too, without your being able to control it. By assigning the cause to someone else, another person, the event becomes something that can be evaded.[49] Therefore, the bias serves the individual's own wellbeing and is the result of individual motives.[50]

Psychology Quarterly 1985, Vol. 48, No.3. pp. 227-236, particularly p. 228 and Vonk *et al.* 2007, p. 44 and pp. 203-207.

46 *See* for example J.H. Harvey *et al.*, 'How Fundamental is "The Fundamental Attribution Error"?', *Journal of Personality and Social Psychology* 1981, Vol. 40, No. 2, pp. 346-349 and the response by G.D. Reeder, 'Let's Give the Fundamental Attribution Error Another Chance', *Journal of Personality and Social Psychology* 1982, Vol. 43, No. 2, pp. 341-344.

47 For more details *see* Vonk *et al.* 2003, pp. 124-128.

48 *See* Vonk *et al.* 2003, p. 139; *see also* Hans & Dee 2002-2003, pp. 1103 *et seq.* and Barendrecht 2004, pp. 55-56.

49 In that respect this theory looks like the so-called 'just world hypothesis', *see, e.g.*, Van Koppen 2010, pp. 23 *et seq.*

50 Vonk *et al.* 2003, p. 139; J.M. Burger, 'Motivational Biases in the Attribution of Responsibility for an Accident: A Meta-Analysis of the Defensive-Attribution Hypothesis', *Psychological Bulletin* 1981, Vol. 90, No. 3, pp. 497-498 and p. 510; Farnsworth 2007, p. 242, and A.E. Stewart, 'Attributions of Responsibility for Motor Vehicle Crashes', *Accident Analysis and Prevention* 2005, Vol. 37, p. 682. This also explains why rape victims often blame themselves, because being responsible for it yourself means that the event can be avoided (in the future), *see* the overview in Burger 1981, p. 497. *See also* Farnsworth 2007, p. 242.

This bias has been subjected to further studies. One of the discoveries was that it is difficult to find confirmation for this bias and so it was modified as follows: when the observer judges someone else's responsibility, the attribution may be distorted if the observer and actor are very much alike and the actor is in a situation the observer could also be in. So the similarities between the actor and the observer, as well as the seriousness of the result contribute to defensive attribution.[51]

As far as the similarities between the actor and observer are concerned: the similarities will occur if the observer (could or) will face the same situation as the actor in the future. Subsequently, the observer will seek to deny the personal similarities. If this fails, he may resort to other strategies such as the attribution to coincidence, and not to the person who is not so different from the observer himself, or the consequences are minimized. This is how the observer ensures that he will not or cannot be the one to blame for any future accident in which he may be involved.[52]

If, however, the observer does not see any similarities, meaning he does not regard himself as a potential actor but rather as a victim, he will not be willing to assign the event to coincidence.[53] Our assessment of a person with whom we share certain traits tends to be milder than our assessment of a person who does not display these similarities. Subsequently, it was also confirmed that if the observer is similar to the actor and the situation is the same, the attribution to that actor will be less, even more so when the consequences are more serious.[54] If there are no situational or personal similarities, however, more responsibilities are assigned to the actor if the gravity of the consequences is greater (the original theses of defensive attribution).[55] The idea is, again, that if it is not a matter of chance, a serious event can be evaded, can be controlled.

2.3.4 Actor-Observer Differences

The previous observations addressed the attribution by someone who is observing the actor. This situation can and should be distinguished from the case in which the attribution by the actor himself is at issue. After all, the observer focuses on the actor (who is salient, see para. 2.3.2), but the actor himself is not able to focus on that, so he will focus on the situation as it appears to him. As the actor himself will be particularly focused on his environment – which is, after all, salient for him – the attribution of his own conduct will then be too-strongly focused on that environment (*i.e.*, too

51 Burger 1981, p. 498; Stewart 2005, p. 682. *See* (for whiplash cases) Hans & Dee 2002-2003, p. 1103.

52 Burger 1981, p. 498.

53 Burger 1981, pp. 498-499.

54 The victim is even held responsible, *see* Hans & Dee 2002-2003, p. 1105.

55 Hans & Dee 2002-2003, p. 1106.

much external attribution). The difference between the attribution of an individual's own behaviour and that of others is called the actor-observer difference.[56] The explanation for this can be found in the differences in observation and the fact that the actor has more information available about his own situation.[57]

The cause of this difference in perception can probably be found in the understanding (the knowledge) of the situation, as mentioned earlier (in para. 2.3.2); while the observer sees the acting person, the actor himself sees the environment and that creates, literally, a different perspective. If we were to adjust these positions, for example by placing the actor in front of a mirror or by asking the observer to try and place himself in the actor's position (to create empathy) the difference in attribution is also reduced.[58] As the existence of the actor-observer distortion as such has recently been brought up for a principle discussion, we will have to use this 'adjustment' with caution, however.[59]

2.3.5 Self-Serving Bias

'People are more likely to make self-attributions for positive than for negative outcomes', according to the self-serving bias.[60] Success is particularly and sooner assigned to internal factors (such as someone's ability and effort), whereas failure is attributed to external factors such as the difficulty of the job, someone else's errors and bad luck. This is how we can preserve our self-confidence and self-conceit. It is in the interest of the individual.[61]

Thus this bias has two components. The first is self-defence: people do not assign the cause of negative events (failure) to themselves. The second is self-enhancement:

56 *See* on this in particular E.E. Jones & R.E. Nisbett, *The Actor and the Observer: Divergent Perceptions on the Causes of Behavior*, Morristown: General Learning Press, especially p. 15; R.E. Nisbett *et al.*, 'Behavior as Seen by the Actor and as Seen by the Observer', *Journal of Personality and Social Psychology* 1973, Vol. 27, No. 2, pp. 154-164; D. Watson, 'The Actor and the Observer: How are Their Perceptions of Causality Divergent?', *Psychological Bulletin* 1982, Vol. 92, No. 3, pp. 682-700 and furthermore, among others, Vonk *et al.* 2007, pp. 207-208; Vonk *et al.* 2003, pp. 131-132; Van Koppen 2010, pp. 19-20; Plous 1993, p. 181.

57 *See* for example Watson 1982, p. 683.

58 Vonk *et al* 2003, p. 132, and in more detail Jones & Nisbett 1971, p. 5 *et seq.*, and pp. 9-10, and also for example M.D. Storms, 'Videotape and the Attribution Process', *Journal of Personality and Social Psychology* 1973, Vol. 27, No. 2, pp. 165-175; D.T. Regan & J. Totten, 'Empathy and Attribution: Turning Observers into Actors', *Journal of Personality and Social Psychology* 1975, Vol. 32, No. 5, pp. 850-856 and R.E. Galper, 'Turning Observers into Actors: Differential Causal Attributions as a Function of "Empathy"', *Journal of Research in Personality* 1976, 10, pp. 328-335.

59 *See* Malle 2006, especially p. 907.

60 Plous 1993, p. 185; Vonk *et al.* 2003, p. 137. *See also* Vonk *et al.* 2007, pp. 131-134, and Farnsworth 2007, p. 243.

61 *See* Weiner 1986, p. 300 and Vonk *et al.* 2003, p. 137.

people think they themselves are responsible for positive results (success).[62] This distortion does not occur, though, when the other person is someone with whom one has a bond because people want to maintain the positive self-image of the other person.[63]

The existence of this bias has been the subject of a fierce discussion though, which is not over yet.[64] It implies we have to proceed with caution here. Moreover, we should not forget that this error is (also) understandable and functional. After all, always assigning failure to yourself and success to external factors could be paralysing. It can lead to not achieving anything at all in the long run.[65]

2.3.6 Interim Conclusion

There are more distortions or errors related to attribution theory, such as the egocentric bias. A person accepts more responsibility for a result achieved jointly than the other participants assign to this individual.[66] Also think of augmentation, the reverse of the discounting principle mentioned earlier (para. 2.3.1).[67] It means that the facilitating cause of certain acts (the cause that smoothes the way for the act to take place) is regarded as more dominant if there is also an inhibitive factor. If you persevere in your divorce, in spite of the loss of luxury, your home situation must indeed have become unbearable.[68] Furthermore, I will just mention the positivity effect,[69] the way we process new information and the way we use stereotypes,[70] and the recently-claimed sexual attribution bias.[71] I will ignore these as the previous observations have already

62 The mirror of this internal attribution of your own success and the external attribution of your own failure is that someone else's success is attributed externally and someone else's failure attributed internally (to that individual).
63 Vonk *et al.* 2003, p. 137.
64 *See* on this Ross & Anderson 1982, pp. 133-135 and, for example, Th.S. Duval & P.J. Silvia, 'Self-Awareness, Probability of Improvement, and the Self-Serving Bias', *Journal of Personality and Social Psychology* 2002, Vol. 82, No. 1, particularly p. 49 and p. 57 (the attribution in case of a failure remains particularly unclear).
65 Vonk *et al.* 2003, pp. 137-138 and p. 141.
66 Plous 1993, pp. 185-186. This also occurs with undesired (negative) results, such as the cause of a marital row.
67 Vonk *et al.* 2003, pp. 96-97; *see also* Shaver 1985, pp. 54-56 and Van Koppen 2010, p. 17. The role played by the causal factor in discounting is always considered smaller if there are also other facilitating causes.
68 Vonk *et al.* 2003, pp. 96-97. Or, but that is much more speculative: if a supervisor as secondary wrongdoer failed to supervise and damage is suffered after someone else, the primary wrongdoer, acted this act must have been very determining (very strong causal contribution in the assessment of the acts of both wrongdoers).
69 Plous 1993, p. 186.
70 Van Koppen 2010, pp. 21-22.
71 F. Fösterling *et al.*, 'Ability, Luck, and Looks: An Evolutionary Look at Achievement Ascriptions and the Sexual Attribution Bias', *Journal of Personality and Social Psychology* 2007, Vol. 92, No. 5, pp. 775-788.

provided enough food for thought. Which of all these distortions or biases discussed earlier affects or could affect (our dealings with) the law, particularly regarding the decisions made with respect to causation issues and how? And if such effects are present, should we or must we do something about it and if yes, what?

2.4 Back to the Legal Appraisal

2.4.1 Decisions on Causation

Now that I have described the legal as well as the psychological view on the theme of the assignment of causes, the question arises how good or bad the link is between the legal and psychological field. As I primarily focus on the legal aspects of causation issues in this paper, the issue narrows down to what lawyers – whereby I will particularly focus on the civil law judge's perspective or that of the citizen seeking justice – could learn if they were to take the newly-provided perspective to heart.

Well, judges cut the Gordian knot; they are the people who make and must make decisions. And even before that, the parties' lawyers, during the litigation or settlement process, wonder about the decision the judge is probably going to make and in order to do that they place themselves in the judge's position. Is there enough evidence to support the *condicio sine qua non* argument? Will item of loss x or y be compensated?

Any distortions or biases, regardless of their nature, on the decisions of people in general then also become highly relevant for judges and advocates alike. In order to reach the right decisions, these biases should be eliminated as much as possible or at least be allowed for in the sense that one is aware of and takes into account the possibility of mistakes being made. Examples are, apart from the attribution theories discussed in this paper, the studies which have shown that laypeople serving as jurors are less likely to accept liability if the causal chain between accident and damage is more complex, has more chains or when more time has passed between the behaviour and the damage, whereas these are factors that are legally irrelevant.[72] Of course, judges in civil cases must also bear this in mind when they assess the causal chain.

The 'errors' made by judges and others related to the attribution of causes to persons or events are all the more relevant in this context as private law abounds with assess-

72 *See* J.T. Johnson & J. Drobny, 'Proximity Biases in the Attribution of Civil Liability', *Journal of Personality and Social Psychology* 1985, Vol. 48, No. 2, pp. 283 *et seq.*; T. Wayte *et al.*, 'Psychological Issues in Civil Law', *in*: J.R.P. Ogloff, *Taking Psychology and Law into the Twenty-First Century*, New York: Kluwer 2002, p. 347.

ments on causal relationships. After all, judges are required at all times to uncover causal relationships and assess them, not only regarding tort law which is my focus of attention in this paper, but also outside of tort law, for example when a party relies on the doctrine of 'mistake'.

The method of attribution people use, as described above, should impress on us that judges (and advocates) often and probably make mistakes when they assess causal relationships. Note that this is certainly not meant to reproach the judiciary or the bar; all it means is that judges and advocates are human and fallible, just like the rest of us. This does not mean, however, that we can or should leave it at this. We must be willing to learn from our attribution errors, whenever possible.

2.4.2 Clues for the Improvement of the Rules or their Application?

2.4.2.1 Introduction

What we can and should do about this kind of errors is simply the following.[73] We will have to seek to eliminate the biases or at least try to reduce them; we will have to go into 'debiasing'. And while we are considering this, we will also have to examine whether we need other or better legal rules than the ones we have now. I will focus, in the first instance, on the rules regarding causation, but I cannot avoid addressing also the legal system (including procedural law) as such.

2.4.2.2 Debiasing the Fundamental Attribution Error

The fundamental attribution error, the tendency to assign the cause of an event to the acting individual and underestimate factors outside of that individual (the rest of the situation) may lead to an assessment of causal connections in which the decision maker, the judge, the observer, looks at the acting individual in particular, as a result of which the latter will dominate instead of the situation. The difference in result can be substantial: are this person's properties to blame or is it his environment?[74]

We are able, however, to eliminate this fundamental 'error' by paying close attention to 'consensus information' (what do other people do?). After all, in such a case (when everyone is acting the same) an explanation based on the properties of an acting individual is not very likely. Moreover, we will have to look for hidden causes, the causes that are not obvious or salient.[75] The latter may happen spontaneously when

73 I will ignore the issue whether it is the legislator or the judge who should act here. According to J.J. Rachlinski, 'Bottom-up versus Top-down Lawmaking', *in*: Gigerenzer & Engel 2006, pp. 159 *et seq.*, such depends on the circumstances.

74 *See also* Plous 1993, p. 183, and especially in relation to accident law and the role in lawyers in that regard, Feigenson 1995.

75 Plous 1993, p. 187 and p. 188.

the observer thinks that the acting individual has a hidden agenda. In such cases we really start thinking about the behaviour, which will weaken the distortion. In fact, thinking longer and harder can reduce this fundamental attribution error and the requirement (known beforehand) to account for and explain the choices made, has been shown to be able to prevent it from occurring.[76] The same applies when we focus on the situation instead of the person, but then there is a risk that we overshoot the mark.[77]

The focus and reflection on the case as a whole, including the situation as well as the actors, can be encouraged, in my view, by making sure that the focus of the judge is spread, by encouraging those involved to consider other causes as well. This is precisely what I think can be achieved (as, indeed, we would then consider more than one cause) by applying, from a technical-legal point of view, the doctrine of proportional liability, which is for example used these days in the Netherlands[78] in the field of liability for asbestos-related diseases and discussed elsewhere in Europe.[79] After all, in these cases all possible known causal contributions (such as the exposure to dangerous substances, like asbestos, but also smoking and the known environmental factors and risks) must be incorporated in the assessment, as they are part of it. As a result, each cause can be considered on its own merit. Judges will have to think long and hard about the assessment of the causal connections of all these factors and that may prevent or reduce the chance of attribution errors being made.[80]

Apart from this, admittedly, rather speculative idea, the following also applies here. A judge who is asked to assess causal connections must try to look beyond the person and also consider the situation. It may be an advantage in this case that civil

76 *See* on the last subject, Tetclock 1985, especially p. 232 and p. 233. If an individual is required to give an account of his choices, the attribution error is diminished. This is particularly the case when it is known beforehand that this will be required.

77 Vonk *et al.* 2003, pp. 128-130; Vonk *et al.* 2007, p. 206; Harvey *et al.* 1981, p. 347.

78 *See, e.g.,* Dutch Supreme Court 31-3-2006, *NJ* 2011, 50 (*Karamus/Nefalit*) and the many comments related to it, such as I. Giesen & T.F.E. Tjong Tjin Tai, *Proportionele Tendensen in het Verbintenissenrecht*, Deventer: Kluwer 2008, with many references to earlier studies on the phenomenon of proportional liability. Of course, 'other possible causes' will also be considered, if, for example, a decision has to be made on the distribution of the cost when there are a number or parties who are jointly and severally liable.

79 On (the discussion about) proportional liability outside the Netherlands, *see*, *e.g.*, Th. Kadner Graziano, 'Loss of a Chance in European Private law', *European Review of Private Law* 2008, pp. 1022 *et seq.*; J. Taupitz, 'Proportionalhaftung zur Lösung von Kausalitätsproblemen: Insbesondere in der Arzthaftung?', *in*: A. Heldrich (u.a.) (hrg.), *Festschrift für Claus-Wilhelm Canaris zum 70. Geburtstag*, München: Beck 2007, pp. 1231 *et seq.*; M.D. Green, 'The future of Proportional Liability: the Lessons of Toxic Substances Causation', *in*: M. Stuart Madden, *Exploring Tort Law*, Cambridge: Cambridge University Press 2005, pp. 352 *et seq.* and Art. 3:103 of the Principles on European Tort Law (PETL).

80 Part of the judge's assessment is that he may also incorporate the degree of blame by virtue of Arts. 6:98, 101 and 102 CC, which presents an additional pitfall. *See* below.

proceedings (at least on the continent, in civil law jurisdictions) are to a large extent conducted in writing, and only become 'alive' on paper since the paperwork detracts the observer's (the judge's) focus from the actor. It may make for 'improved' (less extreme) assessments of all the relevant factors. If this fails and, as a result, the dispositional factors outweigh the rest,[81] this may become manifest in wrongly assuming a high degree of fault, one of the imputation factors, which can lead to an imputation that is too broad in the sense of Article 6:98 BW. This does not mean that this legal rule is wrong – far from it, there is a lot to be said for the idea of more strictness when someone has committed a major mistake – but its application must remain a point of attention.

As far as the injured party's own fault (contributor negligence[82]) is at issue, the foregoing may also play a role since that assessment is about weighing the (amount of) responsibility and thus the causal contributions of both parties (tortfeasor and victim). After that initial causal assessment, these considerations can be 'corrected' or mitigated by also looking at the respective degrees of fault or blame of both parties. But this is a possible pitfall again, since this may go wrong if the actor receives too much attention. The fact that, for example, the Dutch Supreme Court has broadened the margin of discretion of lower courts, by laying down only very limited requirements regarding the motivation of their decision on contributory negligence – as this is supposedly an intuitive[83] assessment – is certainly not helpful to prevent such pitfalls.[84] The same remark could be made in relation to English law since the same 'leniency' towards the motivation of lower court judgments, who, after all, are giving a judgment on the facts, seems to exist in England.[85]

81 This may happen, for example, because the civil judge only actually sees the parties on rare occasions, such as during the personal appearance of the parties to give information or reach a settlement and during the oral pleadings at the end of the trial phase. This means there is little experience with these parties and so there is little information and then the attribution fails, *see* Van Koppen 2010, p. 19.

82 *See, e.g.*, §254 German Civil Code; Section 1(1) of the Law Reform (Contributory negligence) Act 1945; Art. 6:101 Dutch Civil Code; Art. 5:102 PEL Liab.Dam.; Arts. 8:101 and 3:106 PETL, and the comparative overviews in Von Bar 2005, Chapter 5, Art. 5:102, Comments and Notes (pp. 808 *et seq.*); Van Dam 2006, nos. 1212-1215; Van Gerven *et al.* 2000, pp. 689-728; J. Spier, *Schadevergoeding: Algemeen, Deel 3. Mon. Nieuw BW (B36)*, Deventer: Kluwer 1992, pp. 5-8. *See also* Viney/Jourdain 2006, nos. 425-1 *et seq.*, on French law which has no code provision on this topic. However, for French law, the Arts. 3-5 of the *Loi Badinter* (Loi no 85-677; the act dealing with road traffic liability) are especially important in this regard.

83 On the importance of intuition in judicial decision making: W. van Rossum, 'Vier Reflecties op Empirisch Onderzoek naar Rechterlijke Oordeelsvorming', *NJB* 2010, pp. 2467-2472.

84 *See* in general Hartkamp *et al.* 2009, no. 124, and cases such as the Dutch Supreme Court 4-5-2001, *NJ* 2002, 214 (*Chan-a-Hung/Maalsté*), at 3.7.4.

85 *See* Rogers 2006, p. 332: 'the judges give little by way of reason for their assesments' because the issue 'is commonly treated as a matter of fact'.

The absence, in these systems, of a necessity to provide proper arguments underlying the outcome, will most probably not contribute to more and more thorough reflections on this issue, which is the very thing that would be required from the psychological point of view. Thinking longer and harder can reduce fundamental attribution errors and the requirement (known beforehand) to account for and explain the choices made, has been shown to be able to prevent them from occurring.[86] After all, the motivation makes choices transparent. As this idea also means that the judicial motivation of a decision must meet high(er) standards, this part of the law must be adjusted. This would only be different if the judiciary were to make no or fewer attribution errors, but as far as we can tell there are no indications to assume this.[87]

2.4.2.3 What to Do with the Codified Defensive Attribution Bias

The bias of defensive attribution can be used (or should we say: misused) in systems which still use juries[88] by making sure and emphasising that the members of such a jury and the plaintiff in for instance cases such as traffic accidents, are very similar. A jury consisting of members who have been victims of traffic accidents themselves would be the preferred choice for the victim in such a case. Those jury members will not assign their past accident to themselves, nor to the victim, as a result thereof.[89] His opponent and society will obviously have very different views on the 'desirability' of the composition of the jury.

Most European legal systems, with professional judges instead of juries, however, do not work like this. Here we have to make sure that there is no 'identification' between a litigating party and the judge (same social background, same social environment?), which could make the judge's view on that party's causal contribution more lenient. The judge must be impartial and independent, we say, and that is why the system lays down safeguards. It is my view that the required intervention by advocates on both sides leads to the aversion of many calamities. After all, judges will sense a certain

86 *See* on the last subject, Tetclock 1985, especially p. 232 and p. 233. If an individual is required to give an account of his choices, the attribution error is diminished. This is particularly the case when it is known beforehand that this will be required. Judges know, obviously, before they reach a decision that at some moment in time a motivation is needed.

87 After all, judges (and advocates) make decisions in a state of uncertainty, which means errors are made because they, too, are influenced by several biases. *See* Giesen 2005a, p. 92, n. 290. *See* on this subject in a broader context P.J. van Koppen & J.W. de Keijser, 'Beslissende Rechters', *in*: P.J. van Koppen *et al.* (Eds.), *Reizen met mijn Rechter*, Deventer: Kluwer 2010, pp. 861 *et seq.*, and also W.A. Wagenaar, H.F.M. Crombag & H. Israëls, 'Ook Rechters Maken Menselijke Fouten', *in*: P.J. van Koppen *et al.* 2010, pp. 875 *et seq.* I do not know, however, of any hard figures showing that judges in civil cases, as a specific group, make (many) attribution errors.

88 On decision making by juries *see*, *e.g.*, Feigenson 1995 and specifically on juries and damage awards, *see* E. Greene *et al.*, 'Jurors and Juries', *in*: J.R.P. Ogloff, *Taking Psychology and Law into the Twenty-First Century*, New York: Kluwer 2002, pp. 240 *et seq.*, and Wayte *et al.* 2002, pp. 348 *et seq.*

89 Hans & Dee 2002-2003, pp. 1115-1117.

feeling of equality towards both advocates (at least they have all read law as a student) which means that any effect is 'shared' by both parties.

The judge must, however, be extra attentive in those (seemingly safe) situations where there are no situational and personal similarities between him and the litigating parties. The judge's open-mindedness which is simply assumed to be present in such cases is not obvious. After all, in those cases more responsibility will be assigned to the actor if the seriousness of the consequences is greater, which means that there is a chance that the causal consequences of a negligent act will be imputed to a too large extent to the tortfeasor if it actually concerns a serious form of negligence with serious consequences.

This is, in essence, exactly what, for instance, the PETL, but also Dutch legislation and case law allow to happen. After all, the law as it now stands enables the imputation of the damage and loss to the liable individual to be dependent on the nature of the damage, whereby this imputation can be more extensive in case of bodily injuries (such injuries are regarded as more serious, which requires this extended imputation, *see* para. 2.2.1). The law therewith allows the imputation to be more extensive if the actual cause is the same as in a similar event without such injuries.[90] This means that defensive attribution has been codified, as it were, in our tort law. This effect is strengthened furthermore by the rule regarding the extensive imputation in cases of traffic or safety norm violations since these cases also concern bodily injuries, which implies that the consequences are more serious. It means that judges are invited, once again, to use a distortion regarding the imputation of causes to behaviour.

Note that this does not suddenly make the present rules on imputation wrong, as these rules may be well indicated owing to normative considerations (such as stricter sanctions if the consequences are more serious; the principle of full compensation). Therefore my opinion on the pros or cons of these legal rules as such (which enjoy strong support among lawyers) is not relevant here. I do want to say, however, that given the previous observations, we should proceed with caution when we apply these rules and ask ourselves the question whether the imputation does not go too far. Fortunately, this aspect is also one of the factors that are part of the assessment of Article 6:98 BW.

90 Think for example of two cases in which boys playing football break a window. If the first case leads to injury and the second one does not, the imputation will be more extensive in the first case, whereas the causal relation (cause and effect) is, in essence, the same.

2.4.2.4 Actor and Observer: Emphatic Judges

As discussed, there is a difference in attribution depending on the question whether this concerns someone else's behaviour or the actor's. If the observer were to take the place of the actor (partly) by putting himself in the other person's position (in other words: to show empathy), the difference in attribution disappears. The other individual's act (those of the actor), is more often imputed by the observer to the environment (external attribution, just like the actor would do himself) than is the case with attribution of the conduct of someone else who is just being observed.[91] The result is that the fundamental attribution error is reduced.[92]

This may also be of importance for the legal assessment. After all, if the observer (read: the judge) must or is willing and able to imagine himself in the situation of the actor, which means he shows empathy, he will have more consideration for the environment as a factor of causality. This reduces the distortion of the fundamental attribution error (assigning the conduct too much to personal characteristics). At first sight this seems to lead to a more-balanced assessment of each individual's causal contribution. Therefore there does not seem to be any harm when a judge puts himself, to a certain extent, in the position of the person addressed. When doing so (*see* para. 2.4.2.2), it turns out that judges think longer and harder. It would appear that empathic judges produce more-balanced judgments.[93]

2.4.2.5 The Self-serving Bias and the Acceptance of Negative Results

The self-serving bias discussed earlier may also have consequences for some legal issues. After all, the imputation of damage or loss to the tortfeasor will not always be sufficiently understood by him. As a result of this distortion, this actor will not easily attribute the negative result of certain acts (damage) to himself. At best, he will accept the result with difficulty as it does not match his own image.[94]

Obviously, the civil judge may be able to enforce that 'acceptance' by the person addressed, in the sense that he provides the other party with a title to enforcement of his judgment, but this bias will already have made the negotiations on the settlement

---

91 *See* para. 2.3.4; Regan & Totten 1975, and Vonk *et al.* 2003, p. 132.

92 One has to proceed with caution when linking both distortions, *see* B.F. Malle, 'The Actor-Observer Asymmetry in Attribution: A (Surprising) Meta-Analysis', *Psychological Bulletin* 2006, Vol. 132, No. 6, p. 896.

93 On this theme earlier already I. Giesen, 'Rechtspraak Is Mensenwerk', *Recht der Werkelijkheid* 2003-1, pp. 39 *et seq.* (with a response from Kerkmeester on pp. 45 *et seq.*). It must be said here that a judge, and that is the hard part of his work, must not identify himself too much with the victim because that can lead to underestimating the victim's contribution too much.

94 To this we must add that owing to the 'actor-observer bias' (*see* para. 2.3.4), parties may disagree on the interpretation of an event such as a traffic accident, *see* S.R. Wilson *et al.*, 'Attribution Complexity and Actor-Observer Bias', *Journal of Social Behavior and Personality* 1997, Vol. 12, No. 3, p. 710.

of the claim more difficult.[95] Moreover, after the court's decision this bias may lead to an increased willingness on the part of the person addressed to lodge an appeal.

Preventing this error would be a bonus, considering the previous observations as more extra-judicial settlements and fewer appeal cases would save the parties costs[96] and reduce the judiciary's workload, but it is also very difficult. Debiasing is possible, though, because the self-serving bias is less strong if there is a bond with the other individual, but in tort law that is typically not the case. The parties concerned were not acquainted before the accident. To try and make the parties bond afterwards seems to be a sensible thing to do. It will not have adverse effects on the mutual acceptance and may even help it. That is perhaps also the reason why mediation, once initiated, often succeeds.

2.4.3 Interim Conclusion

The previous observations demonstrate how, in a limited number of situations, the attribution errors discussed earlier may affect legal issues and, subsequently, which remedies we have available (or must have). In addition to this, I could have pointed out that the degree of perceived responsibility of an individual increases if his acts are intentional.[97] This thought fits in very well with our present theories on causation since the degree of fault (intent indicates a large degree of fault) plays a role in the imputation on the basis of Article 6:98 BW. This sub-rule (this is one of the factors of causal imputation) is thus well-chosen even though the very same consideration may also carry a certain risk (see para. 2.4.2.2). The latter is still of importance: it is not at all easy to attune psychology and rules of law to each other, but things will become even more difficult when contrary forces (distortions) are at work. The advantages that may be gained with this are such, however, that it is worthwhile making the effort.

2.5 The Effect of Attribution on the Intended Behavioural Effect?

Before I come to the conclusion of this paper, there is still one last issue that must be addressed. In paragraph 2.2.2, I already addressed the aim of tort law (including its rules on causation) to prevent the potential tortfeasor to commit any damaging acts and to cause damage to another individual. So far, I have assumed that this so-called

95 In more detail L. Babcock & G. Loewenstein, 'Explaining Bargaining Impasse: The Role of Self-serving Biases', *in*: C.R. Sunstein (Ed.), *Behavioral Law and Economics*, New York: Cambridge UP 2000, pp. 355 *et seq*.

96 *See* Babcock & Loewenstein 2000, pp. 362. Earlier experience with negotiations does not annul the bias (pp. 362-363 and p. 367).

97 Vonk *et al.* 2003, p. 88.

preventive effect is present, at least to a certain extent.[98] The psychological views presented above also lead, in my view, to the deduction that attribution theory, the ideas on how people impute causes to persons or events, is essential for the answer to the question whether the intended behavioural effect of tort law can actually exist and does exist. The argument is as follows.

If the actor (in this case: the injured party, the person addressed) imputes the cause of a certain event (the event causing the damage) to himself, if he attributes the event internally, and if he does so with the (unconscious) aim of learning from earlier experiences (which is one of the reasons why persons attribute, para. 2.3.1), then my conclusion would be that the actor will act with more caution in the future (special prevention). And if he then tells his story to the people around him, this will also have a general preventive effect, I presume.[99] Since the method of (internal) attribution determines the learning effect and prevention here, and even though there is no input from tort law (which basically has nothing to do with this), the intended behavioural effect of tort law may yet be achieved (though by a different method) as the learning effect is in itself achievable.[100]

If the actor, however, imputes the event to another person or the local situation at the moment when the event occurred, if he attributes 'externally', the actor will also think that he goes scot-free as far as the cause of the damage is concerned. Thus, there is no reason to adjust his behaviour in the future and to act with more caution. The intended behavioural effect will not manifest itself and there is nothing tort law can do to change this. Tort law has no preventive effects as (stronger) attribution mechanisms prevent or annihilate any possible learning effects in advance.

When we link all this to the notion that people tend to attribute events to another individual (rather than to themselves) if the conduct in question has more serious consequences ('defensive attribution', para. 2.3.3) and particularly to the thought that success is attributed internally while failure is attributed externally (para. 2.3.5, the self-serving bias), the obvious conclusion would be that acts which cause damage – often behaviour with serious consequences which must be qualified as a failure – will lead to external attribution and therefore fail to have the intended behavioural effect. One will explain away one's own behaviour and will not be willing to learn.

---

98 *See, generally* on prevention (deterrence) and psychology, J. Darley, S. Fulero & C. Haney *et al.*, 'Psychological Jurisprudence', *in*: J.R.P. Ogloff, *Taking Psychology and Law into the Twenty-First Century*, New York: Kluwer 2002, pp. 37 *et seq*.

99 However, the empirical basis of this presumption should be examined.

100 It is difficult, anyway, to make any firm (or firmer) statements on this as the influence of the so-called consensus information on the attribution is not obvious, *see* para. 2.3.1.

This conclusion is of major importance. The idea unfolded here forms, in my view, a possible explanation for the often suggested lack of preventive effect of tort law. When people attribute events externally there is no didactic effect. That attribution is too strong; tort law cannot compete with it.[101] Earlier events therefore will not lead to prevention of damage and this confirms the doubts on the preventive effect of tort law.

This explanation becomes even stronger, in my view, when we also incorporate the distinction that is often made by academic lawyers between the preventive effect when it concerns 'one-shotters', namely the private person or consumer who rarely faces the consequences of tort law or 'repeat players', such as companies who make their considerations regarding liability part of their decisions.[102] According to these academics, the preventive effect of tort law is stronger in the second case. This image matches the previous observations to the extent that the first group (the one-shotters) may be expected to attribute more externally because their own personal conduct is at issue (in other words: their self-image), whereas the second group (the institutionalized defendants) attribute the error they made internally within their organization as this does not concern an individual whose feelings of self-confidence are affected. The organization as a whole, the company, and not a particular individual, takes the 'blame' and points to itself as the guilty party. This organization may also be expected to act more rationally and to consider it important to learn from mistakes made in the past, which implies that this organization will sooner attribute internally than an individual does.[103]

2.6 Conclusion

The aim of this paper was to examine whether attribution as a psychological phenomenon fits in with the notion of causal imputation in the legal sense, and if not, whether both concepts can be aligned to some extent. The conclusion is that both concepts are not simply compliant. Therefore we should proceed with caution when we make decisions on causation issues and try to take into account the lessons from attribution theory. In addition to specific suggestions for improvements it has be-

101 This may be different (but I am now speculating) if the damages awarded to compensate for negligent behaviour are so weighty that an individual will learn from it anyway (tort law then contributes to the awareness regarding the attribution error), but it is not clear when that moment sets in and if it is at all achievable. Considering the present degree of insurance coverage and the fact that the wrongdoer will often not directly feel that a payment must be made, the 'learning effect' of tort law must be considered small, in my opinion. Moreover, if someone attributes externally and has to pay anyway he will consider it an unfair 'punishment'.

102 *See* particularly Van Boom 2006 and Giesen 2005b, pp. 148-149, with more references.

103 As to leave no doubts: this last mentioned expectation is one which is not confirmed by specific psychological research, at least not as far as I have been able to find out and it must therefore be regarded in that light.

come clear, in any case, that thinking longer and harder on legal issues when they arise will lead to better answers.[104] That is a valuable lesson.

An even more general and not unimportant lesson to be learnt from the previous observations is that the preventive effects of tort law cannot be (entirely) achieved because attribution mechanisms, as a result of which people mainly attribute certain events externally, may obstruct this. This, in turn, has the consequence that the present educational aspect of tort law only exerts little or no influence.

The broader idea behind this contribution was the very general issue of what tort law should do with the results achieved by psychology. I am of the opinion that the previous has proven, again,[105] that there is so much to learn from psychological research that the link between the two fields should be made more often. It may not make us better lawyers, but it will improve (tort) law.

104 *See* also Babcock & Loewenstein 2000, p. 362: 'considering the opposite' leads to 'debiasing'.
105 *See* already, Giesen 2005a. *See also* Van Rossum 2010, p. 2472 (on the use of psychology in legal training).

3 Facts, Framing and Fallacies in the Tort of Negligence

Raimond W.M. Giard

> Numerous legal judgments, from determining whether a tort defendant failed to take reasonable care to whether a corporate office committed securities fraud by knowingly making false statements, require that a judge or jury ignore what they have learned in hindsight.
> *Jeffrey J. Rachlinski*

3.1 Legal Judgment and the Control of Its Quality

In private law, the task of the legal decision maker is to conclude on a conflict between parties and the procedural rules are there to guarantee a well-structured and fair trial. In tort law an injured party seeks compensation from the person or the organization that committed a wrong. This demands the methodic investigation of what has happened, how that caused damages. Often experts are needed to give their opinion on the case. In order for the judge to fully appreciate and apply all the outlandish information sound legal judgment entails an understanding from the legal decision maker of the interaction between the law and knowledge from other domains.

Judgment is the crucial and concluding step in this complex judicatory process. This decision making is a cognitive process with the emotions from the parties at the background. Next, it is also important to realize that conflicts will always arise in social interactions. All this implies that we should be intrigued by what we can learn from studying these phenomena in order to understand them better, the realms of cognitive and social psychology, as was discussed in chapter 1.

We are confronted here with the chicanery of decision making under uncertainty. This is not a problem that rests exclusively within the legal domain. For example doctors may also come to the wrong diagnosis or choose the inappropriate therapy, CEOs may choose the wrong business strategy, pilots may take an incorrect decision and all this may have disastrous consequences. What can we do to minimize the chance of wrongdoing or even blundering? To start with: We must judge them properly.

For reliable rulings the emphasis will have to be on the examination and optimization of the processes: legal problem solving with information gathering, interpretation and inference. For the proper determination and implementation of these processes within a legal context, more is required than substantive and procedural rules alone. The quest for reliable knowledge, proper thinking and deciding is essential and requires different competences. So, in scrutinizing legal judgment we are confronted with a double normativity, a duplicate 'ought'-ness: we have to incorporate epistemology, the study of the grounds of our knowledge, into legal practice. In this chapter I will dwell more practically on this non-legal dimension of how to acquire reliable knowledge and how to make proper use of it within this particular legal-professional context. How can insights from social and cognitive psychology together with the epistemological notions help us to improve legal judgment? In this chapter I will discuss the reconstruction of past traumatic events with emphasis on examination of the context as one of the major constraints of human decision making. The sufferers from a mishap want a causal explanation and the problems encountered by this venture will be discussed using an analysis of two different tort cases.

3.2 Judging Past Events: The Problem of Reconstruction

Both historians and magistrates are looking at the past, not only to describe but also to understand what has happened and to draw conclusions. After these enquiries, we may understand the past, form an opinion about it, learn from it and perhaps make better decisions in the future. But experiences in both domains show us that different examiners looking back at the same event may come to different conclusions. For historians this may offer them an interesting spectrum of views or an evolution in time of historical insight. But in a legal procedure it is unbearable for the parties involved that his or her fate may depend on who is on the bench. One of the principles of a fair trial is uniformity in the application of the law. However sameness still is no guarantee for rightness. Is it possible to understand why different members of the same discipline may come to different conclusions? Do we have a solution for this problem?

Those who suffered a mishap want an unassailable answer to the question why this set of unfortunate circumstances befell them, they want no less then a proper causal explanation. The legal philosopher Larry Laudan reinforced that once we state that the basic purpose of a trial is the determination of the truth, we have to commit ourselves to what he called 'legal epistemology'.[1] When we follow this line of thought, we are confronted with the pursuit for reliable knowledge. Can we effectively and above all objectively reconstruct the developmental course of the chain of past events? A skeptical attitude is essential for this venture or in the words of the famous French writer and philosopher Michel de Montaigne his lifelong guiding question: 'que sais-je?' ('what do I know?'). Basically we have three seemingly simple but fundamental

1 L. Laudan, Truth, *Error, and criminal law. An essay in legal epistemology*, Cambridge University Press 2006.

questions to answer: what do I know, what should I know and what can I know? But where to start?

3.3 IT IS THE CONTEXT, STUPID!

In tort law, the starting point of a trial always is a nasty event resulting in damages. A tort is a wrong, which entitles the injured party to claim compensation from the person who committed it.[2] Different types of tort exist but in this chapter we will concentrate on the tort of negligence where damages are inflicted through someone's careless action. Most tort cases are about negligence. To bring a claim to a successful end, the victim must show that the tortfeasor owed a duty of care to him or her and acted in a negligent way thereby causing harm.[3] But the tort of negligence has a special difficulty. Negligence is defined by a standard of reasonable care under the given circumstances. It is much too simple to say that the juror has only two successive tasks: fact-finding and applying the law to these facts. The legal norm of reasonable care is a blanket norm. For the negligence decision, a norm creation is needed, an act of discretionary norm creation by the finder of fact.[4] For this purpose, we have to fully appreciate somebody's conduct within a situational context.

The way our lives continuously unfold derives from how we make our decisions. Tort cases may result from actions or inactions based on choices. But how does this overall process of decision making occur? In this activity the context plays a key roll, the set of interrelated conditions in which something exists or occurs. What we perceive is influenced by the surrounding environment, but also by a variety of other elements such as previous experiences, emotions, anticipations, weariness and many other factors. When we review an affair can we reproduce the exact original context in which the disaster took place? It is essential to realize that we can achieve no more than an approximation.[5]

But given the importance of contextual factors, we must do our best to discover as much as we can about the original situation.

If contextual factors have such significant influence on any decision making, this also pertains to legal judgment. These elements may creep in unintentionally but it is also conceivable that lawyers try to induce judges to make judgments in favour of their position. The fundamental lesson form social psychology how to control judgment is

2 J.C.P. Goldberg & B.C. Zipursky, 'Torts as wrongs', *Texas Law Review* 2010, Vol. 88(5), pp. 917-986.

3 D.G. Owen, 'The five elements of negligence', *Hofstra Law Review* 2007, Vol. 35(4), pp. 1671-1687 and J. Oberdiek, 'Philosophical issues in tort law', *Philosophy Compass* 2008, Vol. 3-4, pp. 734-748.

4 K.S. Abrahams, 'The trouble with negligence', *Vanderbilt Law Review* 2001, Vol. 53(1), pp. 1187-1223.

5 P. Croskerry, 'Context is everything or how could I have been that stupid?', *Healthcare Quarterly* 2009, Vol. 12, e171-e177.

that it is often easier to get people to make the decisions that you want by changing the object of judgment than by trying to change their judgment of the object.[6] In the tort of negligence it is the tortfeasor who is the object of judgment and the trial is framed by the unwanted disastrous outcome. Therefore, the presentation of the conflict will guide, or better perhaps: confine, further investigations and inferences. We will now focus on the context of the legal procedure.

3.4 After the Accident: The Victim's Reactions

Let me start with a historic tort case, presented here as a short story, and then analyze how the victims have responded.

> *Case 1.* Jim is a tram driver, who is known to be speeding often. One day, in the town where Jim is working, the weather conditions are grim. A gust of wind topples a tree, which smashes a passing tram – of course driven by Jim. No one is killed, but several passengers were injured. One of them is suing Jim, stating that if Jim had not been speeding, the tram would not have been on the accident spot and nobody would have been hurt.[7]

From the victims perspective there are several characteristic fundamental psychological patterns of reaction when examining past tragedy such as this one. In essence, all these responses regard somebody's demeanour and are consequently social perceptions:

1. The *fundamental surprise* states that for the casualty the occurrence of the calamity is unexpected, it is a complete astonishment – and a very unpleasant one. The trusted view of a fair world is abruptly shattered.[8]
2. The *just world hypothesis* sets out that people have a demand to believe that their environment is a just and orderly place where people usually get what they deserve. We all have a duty of care to maintain this just world. The well-known legal character of the reasonable person should exert all his or hers efforts to keep the world in order (duty of care). So when this just world belief is shattered it must be somebody's fault, such things do not happen erratically and somebody must be held responsible.[9]

6 J.J. Rachlinsky, C. Guthrie & A.J. Wistrich, *Context effects in judicial decision making*, SSRN-paper.
7 *Berry v. Borough of Sugar Notch* (1899) 43 Atl. 240 (Pa.).
8 Z. Lanir, *Fundamental surprise*, Eugene, OR, Decision research 1986 and W. Wagenaar & J. Groeneweg, 'Accidents at sea: multiple causes and impossible consequences', *International Journal of Man-Machine Studies* 1987, Vol. 27, pp. 587-598
9 M.J. Lerner & D.T. Miller, 'Just world research and the attribution process: looking back and ahead', *Psychological Bulletin* 1977, Vol. 85, pp. 1030-1051 and M.J. Lerner, *The belief in a just world: a fundamental delusion*, New York: Plenum 1980.

3. The *fundamental attribution error* is born.[10] In our example it surely must be Jim's fault. The focus is on a personal cause; information about the situation of the misfortune is ignored. People commonly underestimate the degree to which behaviour is externally caused. The observations are focused on people who stand out against situational backgrounds ('behaviour engulfs the field'). Perceptions are enhanced towards personal control and predictability.[11] If it were a persons handling of a situation that was faulty, an alternative action would have saved the situation.
4. This is counterfactual thinking and it may give rise to the *counterfactual fallacy*.[12] Jim did not control the situation properly and hence it could have turned out differently if only he had not been speeding. Counterfactual thinking can enhance perceptions of control and in retrospect we might have done something different to avoid the incident. I will further clarify this subject under paragraph 3.5.
5. This case is also an example of the *conjunction fallacy*: the accident is a compound occurrence and the conjunction of two events – speeding and the tumbling of a tree – are judged as more probable to occur than its constituent events alone.[13] However, probability theory teaches us that the combination of two events can never be more probable than either of those two happenings individually.
6. Finally we have the problem of *judgment in hindsight*. It is a well-known phenomenon in cognitive psychology that adjudication has to be made in hindsight and is hence prone to either *hindsight bias*, a post outcome amplification of the *a priori* predictability of the mishap, or *outcome bias*, the assumption that people must have been uncaring while performing their task.[14]

The psychological reactions of the injured party are those of frustration and anger and the victim blames the tortfeasor for the harm afflicted. The keyword is *indignation*; a term defined from the complex of emotions, beliefs and response tendencies.[15] This indignation results from intuitive moral conviction of the tortfeasors action or inaction and this is consequently expressed as anger. Now a conflict is born. The victim, who is trying to find a causal explanation, is doing so in an emotion-driven but unstructured way, designated by the psychologist Fritz Heider as a 'naïve scientist'.[16]

---

10 E. Jones, 'The rocky road from acts to dispositions', *American Psychologist*, Vol. 34, pp. 107-117.

11 H.R. Riggio & A.L. Garcia, 'The power of situations: Jonestown and the fundamental attribution error', *Teaching of Psychology* 2009, 36, pp. 108-112.

12 D.R. Mandell *et al.* (eds.), *The psychology of counterfactual thinking*, UK: Routledge 2005.

13 A. Tversky & D. Kahneman, 'Extensional versus intuitive reasoning: the conjunction fallacy in probability judgment', *Psychological Review* 1983, Vol. 90(4), pp. 293-315.

14 J. Baron & J.C. Hershey, 'Outcome bias in decision evaluation', *Journal of Personality and Social Psychology* 1988, Vol. 54 pp. 569-579.

15 D. Kahneman & C.R. Sunstein, 'Cognitive psychology of moral intuitions', *Neurobiology and human values* 2005, pp. 91-105

16 B.M. Malle, 'Fritz Heider's legacy. Celebrated insights, many of them misunderstood', *Social Psychology* 2008, Vol. 39(3), pp. 163-173.

The perceptual experience is guiding the sufferer's fact-finding, interpretation and inference. From the victims point of view there is only one interpretation and the accident is henceforth encased in wilful wrongdoing and presented as such. However, others could describe the same reality differently. Each distinctive narration will evoke a different psychological reaction, a process called *framing*. The power of framing is to flip a person into one way of perceiving rather than another. It can produce different responses to what is logically the same problem.[17] Framing effects arise because statements that are extensionally equivalent may nevertheless evoke different associations and different emotional responses.[18] The essence of this negative framing in tort is that it restricts the problem to personal wrongdoing and will thus deflect decision making in the direction of personal wrongdoing away from the context and it may in consequence result in a judgment error.[19] From the perspective of quality control and fair trial it is therefore important to realize that due to a shift in the decision makers' reference points a change in preferences may arise. [20]

If we are striving to find the best possible causal explanation to obtain a righteous verdict, we must oblige ourselves to develop a proper methodology that prevents us from biased and fallacious conclusions. In order to find a causal explanation, we ask why-questions. First, I will explore the more general problem how to determine whether we have formulated proper answers to our why-questions and then focus more specifically on the puzzle of causal explanation within a legal context using a case of presumed medical negligence.

3.5 WHY WE ASK WHY-QUESTIONS AND WHAT DO THEY GIVE US?

Judgment tasks are central to the approach how we understand and experience our world, either personally or professionally. For this comprehension, the answers to our why-questions, we generate possibilities, we form and test hypotheses about the world we meet. We have to rely on particular strategies to formulate and test each of these hypotheses and this may either help us getting things clear or lead us up the wrong road.

17 G. Claxton, *Hare brain, tortoise mind*, London: Fourth Estate 1997, p. 54.

18 C. Sunstein, 'Some effects of moral indignation on law', *Vermont Law Review* 2009, pp. 405-433.

19 J. Jou, J. Shanteau & R.J. Harris, 'An information processing view of framing effects: the role of causal schemas in decision making', *Mem Cognit.* 1996, Vol. 24(1), pp. 1-15.

20 R.A. LeBoeuf & E. Shafir, 'Deep Thoughts and Shallow Frames: On the Susceptibility to Framing Effects', *Journal of Behavioral Decision Making* 2003, 16, pp. 77-92.

3.5.1 Hypothesis Formulation and Testing: How Far Do We Go and How Hard Do We Look?

Whenever we seek an explanation, we may come up with divergent clarifications. Ideally we construct all possible conjectures and gather all the relevant information; then we have to objectively decide which one is the best. We must have enough faith in our conjectures but also we must limit ourselves for practical purposes. 'We are to admit no more causes of natural things than such as are both true and sufficient to explain their appearances' is the advice given by Sir Isaac Newton.[21] In this advice we meet some of the desirable qualities of an explanation: it must be both simple and probable.[22]

How good are we in weighing opposite views? As it turns out in real-life practice, we are not in the business of a well-balanced search for evidence. From the very first moment, we have an unconscious favourite view and subsequently utilize a one-sided approach to hypothesis testing, the positive-test strategy: we prefer to confirm rather than to falsify our suppositions.[23] This strategy implies that we are apt to perform a biased memory search and seek biased evidence in the outside world.[24] We too often refrain from asking truly diagnostic questions. In *bona fide* problem solving it is essential to have a proper problem identification and definition.[25] We must be fully aware of these problems when we are in the process of explanation-based judgment.

3.5.2 Explanation-Based Judgment

If parties are unable to resolve their divergence, the matter will have to be resolved by a court. Then, for the legal juror typical why-questions abound: 'What happened?' 'Why did it happen?' and 'Why is the tortfeasor responsible or not?'. All these issues have to be answered, but the most pertinent of these is the enquiry into the causation of the misadventure. Most legal decisions in tort trials use a general model of *explanation-based judgment.* [26] [27]

21 Sir Isaac Newton, *Philosophiæ Naturalis Principia Mathematica, Book III. Rules of reasoning in philosophy,* 1687.

22 T. Lombrozo, 'Simplicity and probability in causal explanation', *Cognitive Psychology* 2007, Vol. 55, pp. 232-257.

23 J. Klayman & Y-W. Ha, 'Confirmation, disconfirmation, and information in hypothesis testing', *Psychological Review* 1987, Vol. 94(2) pp. 211-228.

24 Z. Kunda, *Social Cognition*, MIT Press 1998, chapter 4 (p. 111).

25 R.J. Sternberg, *Cognitive Psychology*, Wadsworth Cengage Learning 2009, pp. 430-431

26 R. Hoekstra & J. Breuker, 'Commonsense causal explanation in a legal domain', *Artificial Intelligence and Law* 2007, Vol. 15, pp. 281-299.

27 R. Hastie, 'The role of "stories" in civil jury judgments', *Michigan Journal of Law*, 1999 Vol. 32(1), pp. 1-13.

3.5.3 Inference to the Best Explanation

If we are searching for the best possible explanation, we have to formulate criteria for this process of selection. What does the explanation give us? Does it provide true understanding? According to Lipton, three general features of explanation will test this:[28]

a. There is a distinction between knowing that a phenomenon occurs and understanding why it does. Knowing that something is the case and naming it is not enough. Understanding 'why' will require a lot more than knowing 'that'.
b. Are the explanations provided by themselves explained? This feature is also called the why regress. How far can we go back, how deep do we really have to dig and where does it lead to?
c. The possibility of explaining a phenomenon in cases where the phenomenon itself provides an essential part of the reason for believing that the explanation is correct. This is the phenomenon of self-evidencing explanations, the problem of circularity.

These attributes bring together the reason conception of understanding. But we can think of other elements we have to test before we can accept an explanation. Does the explanation fit in a broader scientific view? Is it in line with current schools of thought? Does our understanding of the particular phenomenon fit within a greater collection of similar events? Is the expounding done coherently? But most important is the causal conception of our understanding. But if causation is used to explicate explanation, it too needs further clarification. And we cannot discuss an explanation out of context.[29]

The enquiries of what has happened will often be formulated in the form of a narrative story and we must therefore realize the importance of the way this story is constructed and how the answers on all why-questions are embedded because of that.[30] This will depend heavily on the trial-position of the enquirer (victim, tortfeasor, legal decision maker or expert) and on the setting (in or outside the legal arena). For the fighting parties, the psychology of conflict will prevail, which will bias their interpretations. However, where objectivity is the key word, the legal decision maker insight in factors from cognitive and social psychology and their influence on judgment must have supremacy. After considering the general demands for answering

28 P. Lipton, 'What good is an explanation?', *in*: J. Cornwell (ed.), *Explanations. Styles of explanations in science* Oxford University Press 2004, pp. 1-22.

29 H. Hållsten, 'What to ask of an explanation-theory', *in*: J. Persson and P. Ylikoski (eds.), *Rethinking Explanation*, Springer 2007, pp. 13-26.

30 R. Hastie, 'Conscious and nonconscious cognitive processes in jurors' decisions', *in*: C. Engel & W. Singer (eds.), *Decision making, the human mind*, Cambridge: MIT Press 2008.

why-questions, now is the time to explore the notion of causality when we seek a causal explanation of the event under enquiry.

3.6 CAUSALITY, CAUSATION AND CAUSAL EXPLANATION

It was the Scottish philosopher David Hume (1711-1776) who stated that causality is the cement of the universe. We do not merely passively observe what happens, we generally actively – and often automatically – want to know *why* it happened; we perceive and we then interpret. We infer a causal relation from a mere temporal sequence, the process of inductive reasoning. This may seem straightforward but does it surely provide us with the truth? In tort trials too, we see a sequence of events preceding a disastrous outcome and we spot a decisive step that is identified as *the* causal factor leading to the misfortune – and that crucial phase is always the activity of a person.

What qualifies an explanation as sufficiently causal within a legal context? Is it just a matter of methodical fact-finding and using common sense to interpret what we have found? And what moves us to give credence to an explanation? To understand even simple everyday situations and events, we need a huge amount of 'common-sense' background knowledge.[31] How do we handle more special and complicated conditions such as cases of presumed negligence? In ordinary life once we have perceived a sequence of events, we almost automatically try to identify causal relations between these happenings. If we use the same self-propelling process for clarification of legal questions we must try to capture this customary process. In this way, we may come to very intelligent conclusions but we can also be dead wrong.

Causation is central to every scientific endeavour where we want to unravel the dependency between successive occurrences. Once we have successfully explained why something did happen in the past, we also may fruitfully forecast when something is bound to occur. That is the supposed mechanism underlying how we can learn from our mistakes, because the next time we will choose differently at some crucial point. But this view may be both idealistic and much too simple!

Let us first give a moment's thought to the difference between the concept of causality and that of causation. Understanding the idea of causality and the implications rising from these insights belong to the realm of philosophy, the philosophy of science in particular. This debate on what causality is or isn't is on going for centuries and will

31 R. Hoekstra & J. Breuker, 'Commonsense causal explanation in a legal domain', *Artificial Intelligence and Law* 2007 p. 281.

probably never end; it may even prove to be unsolvable.[32] I mentioned the name of the Scottish philosopher David Hume earlier and he advanced that we cannot reliably infer causation from association, the famous – and notorious – *induction problem*. After we realize the huge problem of solving this ontological-philosophical conundrum of causality, we are next confronted with a very practical problem, that of proving legal causation.

The term 'causation' could in practice be explained as the occurrence of causality and now we must have sensible guidance to solve this puzzle. This might – in theory – be quite simple: for causation two criteria have to be met and these two must stick together like a horse and carriage.[33] First, we need to apply a *counterfactual test*. This counterfactual test demands that we ask whether something would have happened but for the presence (or absence) of a specified factor. Would the tram accident and subsequent injuries not have taken place if only Jim had not been speeding? According to the claimant this is definitely the case. But we could also think of others factors such as the condition of the roots or the trunk of the tree, the weather situation, the construction of the tram carriage, the route of the rails, etcetera. This counterfactual thinking is a vital link in the tort chain.

Second, we need to unravel a *generating mechanism*. This demands that we actually have a process that requires energy to convert one state to another. But did this presumed speeding really bring about the falling of the tree? Would the shrub not have been fallen on top of the tram if the driver was driving at the allowed rapidity? There is no such mechanism involved in this accident so it was a matter of sheer coincidence, not causation from the conduct of the driver.

The mere association of two separate observations and the presumption of a causal relation between them is not enough according to Hume's induction problem. However, the track record of legal judgments shows cases of serious wrong sentencing because legal professionals omitted to take this essential principle that association is not equal to causation into account. An impressive example of this is the problem of birth-associated brain damages. Astronomical amounts have been paid for compensation of parents of these physically and/or mentally handicapped children, especially in the United States, UK and Australia. Many of these children were born after a troublesome delivery and the assumption was made that poor obstetrical care resulted in a prolonged delivery with a low oxygen supply of the child, which resulted in these brain damages. It is a mere association – and statistically a wrong one too!

32 *See* H. Beebee, C. Hitchcock & P. Menzies (eds.), *The Oxford Handbook of causation*, Oxford University Press 2009.
33 S. Sloman, *Causal Models*, Oxford University Press 2005, p. 24.

These legal actions have become very expensive for insurers and described as the 'childbirth litigation industry'.[34] Critical statistical examination however showed that no hard association existed between difficult labour and neurological brain damage; most children born under such conditions were normal and many brain-damaged children had no history of difficult parturition. Furthermore, examination of the pathobiology of this problem has shown that problematic parturition and neurological damage in most cases have the same cause, a group of maternal and infantile factors that combined together produce this very unwanted outcome.[35] The examination and identification of a generic mechanism proved to be decisive. Nevertheless, the counterfactual test was confusing in this case.

3.7 Counterfactual Thinking, Causal Selection

As already stated, when things do turn out abominable, we automatically engage in trying to find out how things happened and how they could have been avoided; these thoughts may even haunt us. We virtually mutate the historical scenario at a specific point and in this new storyline things turn out differently. This response can be seen as an attempt to causally understand what has happened. These counterfactuals that we bring about may increase our emotional responses (emotional amplification) but above all can influence our understanding of the accident to the point of distortion.[36]

The psychologist Roese distinguishes between two kinds of factors.[37] First, there are the factors that will *activate* this type of reasoning. Kahneman and Miller investigated how the sense of 'normality' of an event was experienced.[38] They demonstrated that after an unhappy event a norm is evoked that reflects prior expectancies about it, which differ from the actual outcome and this will generate counterfactual thinking. The seriousness of the event determines how emotional the victim's responses are.

The second class of factors will influence the *content* of what will be mutated. Given the legal background, this is a very crucial point because jurors are explicitly asked to do such counterfactual reasoning: establishing causation demands this type of 'but-

34 I. Blumenthal, 'Cerebral palsy – medicolegal aspects', *Journal of the Royal Society of Medicine* 2001, Vol. 94(12), pp. 624-627.

35 K.B. Nelson, 'Causative factors in cerebral palsy', *Clinical Obstetrics and Gynecology* 2008, Vol. 51(4) pp. 749-762.

36 D.R. Mandel, 'Counterfactuals, emotions, and context', *Cognition and Emotion* 2003, Vol. 17(1), pp. 139-159.

37 B.A. Spellman & A. Kincannon, 'The relation between counterfactual ("but for") and causal reasoning: experimental findings and implications for jurors' decisions', *Law and Contemporary Problems* 2001, Vol. 64(4), pp. 241-264.

38 D. Kahneman & D.T. Miller, 'Norm theory: comparing reality to its alternatives', *Psychological Review* 1986, Vol. 93(2), pp. 136-153.

for' thinking. Since the requirant is driven to seek causal explanations for why and how things could happen, he or she is confronted with various factors or events that could be named as a cause. So, there is the problem of causal selection. How does the victim sort one cause out for the purpose of blame?[39] So, it will be quite important which event will be mutated and how and it is the plaintiff who sets the counterfactual agenda.

Generally, studies of how counterfactual thinking operates suggest the following:[40]

- Earlier events in a story are more mutable than later ones.
- Exceptional or unusual events will be mutated more often than normal or usual ones.
- Events having to do with the focus of the story will be mutated more often than those that do not.
- Personally controllable events will be mutated more often than uncontrollable ones.
- Events perceived as immoral will be mutated often more than moral events.
- The injured party does not perform an exhaustive search for all conceivable counterfactuals.

Since this counterfactual thinking is intended to establish causal attributions and hence will affect liability judgments we must ask: do mutability and causality relate to the same questions? Can we state that what is mutable is equal to what is causal? The focus of counterfactual reasoning is on preventive actions and the focus of causal reasoning is on how an event actually occurred, but they are based on the same information.[41]

Causal relations imply certain counterfactuals, but the critical point is that a causal relation does not imply that events are just related in time to each other, but there is also the necessity of some generating mechanism, as we just saw.[42]

To summarize the above text, we have seen that the victim is driven by moral indignation and that leads to a determined view on what has happened and who is to blame. This judgment may be wrong, incomplete or biased but it is the starting point for the lawsuit. The problem is hence framed into wilful wrongdoing and the

39 D.A. Lagnado & S. Channon, 'Judgments of cause and blame: the effects of intentionality and foreseeability', *Cognition*, 2008, Vol. 108, pp. 754-770.

40 Roese & Spellman.

41 B.A. Spellman, A. Kincannon, & S. Stose, 'The relation between counterfactual and causal reasoning', *in*: D. R. Mandel, D. J. Hilton & P. Catellani (Eds.), *The psychology of counterfactual thinking*, London: Routledge Research 2005.

42 S. Sloman, *Causal Models*, Oxford University Press 2005, pp. 24 *et seq.*

disastrous outcome results from the tortfeasor's unique and enduring dispositions. Knowing this must inspire both the defendants lawyer and the jurors to seek and use a methodology to objectively investigate and judge a tragedy. Let us now apply these insights to the following case.

3.8 A CASE OF A MISSED DIAGNOSIS OF BREAST CANCER

The following case is situated in the context of increasing efforts for the early detection and treatment of cancer in population screening.

> *Case 2.* A 53-year old woman participates for the first time in the Dutch program for population breast cancer screening. Her mammograms are classified as normal. Six months after her screening photos, she feels something lumpy in her left breast and she is referred by her GP to the department of surgery of the local hospital. There a diagnosis of breast cancer is made and she has to undergo cancer surgery. Examination of her resection specimen by the pathologist shows that she has a locally advanced tumor with an unfavourable prognosis particularly because of the many metastatic lymph nodes in her axilla. In spite of optimal local and systemic treatment she dies twenty months later of disseminated breast cancer. Given this late tumor stage her husband cannot believe that there were no abnormalities seen on her screening mammograms. He therefore files a claim against the breast cancer screening centre, stating that the responsible radiologists were negligent because they failed to detect abnormalities.
>
> In the initial phase of the trial, the court appointed an expert radiologist who re-examined the mammograms of the deceased woman. He concludes that there are indeed minor abnormalities to be seen in the left breast, which if noticed would have resulted in complementary diagnostic examinations and probably the detection of the tumor. Based on this testimony, the court decides that the radiologists from the cancer-screening centre were indeed negligent. [43]

In this short case presentation the husbands fundamental surprise and moral indignation are apparent. From a methodological perspective we are confronted with three potentially distorting elements. The first thing that strikes us in this case is the counterfactual thinking by the husband: 'If only the radiologist would have spotted the abnormalities, then chances of cure might have been better.' This hunch of neglect motivates him to start a legal action against the breast cancer-screening centre.

43 Court of Appeal Arnhem, 17 January 2006, LJN AU9962.

This demonstrates the fundamental attribution error where the personal fault is central, neglecting the situation.

So the second thing is that the domain-specific context of this particular type of radiological diagnosis is left out. We should examine this dramatic case from a broader perspective. What is the aim of cancer screening and what is it upshot? Was this an exceptional mishap or does missing a diagnosis in the setting of cancer screening occur more frequent than anticipated and if so: why? Finally the expert examination, the review of the radiographs with outcome knowledge, violates the demands for objective blinded re-examination. For the discussion of these elements, the problem of context and that of outcome bias, we will need to investigate what observational and experimental empirical investigations have learned us on these questions.

3.9 BREAST CANCER SCREENING: ONCE MORE – IT IS THE CONTEXT, STUPID!

The first question that arises is: what is the principle goal of cancer screening? This is the broad medical-scientific context. Cancer population screening is the cyclic diagnostic investigation[44] of men or women in search of a particular cancer, which has not yet manifested itself with either signs or symptoms. Underlying this preventive practice is the assumption that early cancer stands better curative chances when treated than advanced disease.

The initiative for this type of medical intervention is by definition taken by the government who invites people belonging to a certain age group to voluntarily participate in this screening project. This is not a personal action by an individual patient. These invited persons will be tested, *e.g.* undergoing mammography[45] for breast cancer screening, and this serves to discriminate them into one of the following groups: those with an abnormal test indicating the possibility of cancer who will need further work-up and those with a normal test result who will need no further investigations and who will be invited in the next screening round. The aim of screening is not to exclude the presence of the disease in question with certitude but only to select those persons who need further diagnostic assessment of the abnormality found to establish or refute breast cancer by the additional tests.

With proper disease book keeping cancer registries may tell us how many cancers were detected within the screened population group during a defined period (usu-

44 In the Netherlands, women between 50 and 75 years are screened every two years, but in some countries a yearly screening is usual and may start and stop at different ages.

45 Mammography is making X-rays of both breasts and examining these for abnormalities such as abnormal densities or calcifications.

ally several years) and when and how these cancers were detected. Such studies have shown that in a female population screened for breast cancer one out of three breast cancers is found *not* with the screening mammography but between screening rounds, hence they are called 'interval cancers'. So this finding alone shows us that 'missing' breast cancer with mammography is far from incidental, it is instead very common and this phenomenon must be explained.

When it happens, is this invariably because of negligence? The 'normal' test result and the subsequent diagnosis of cancer suggest human error. But we must go behind this designation. The term 'error' is used inconsistently in relation to accidents and described in at least three different ways: error as the cause of failure, error as the failure itself and error as a process.[46] It is much more profitable to define the standards for this type of diagnostic activity and see if any deviation from this standard has occurred.

We must additionally realize that screening for disease in asymptomatic women is fundamentally different from investigating symptomatic women who present themselves with a breast lump. In the latter group, there are always three diagnostic tests applied: palpation (feeling the properties of the lump by the doctor), mammography and finally a needle aspiration or biopsy to obtain cells or tissue for examination. This combination is almost watertight. In the screening situation however there is no such safety net.

The other essential difference is this: the probability of finding disease in a healthy screening population is extremely low – like finding the proverbial needle in a haystack. It is like screening luggage in an airport for explosives or guns. The probability of identifying terrorist's weaponry is minimal. It has been shown experimentally that in these situations of searching for rare abnormalities they are easily missed.[47] This may be a reasonable explanation of the phenomenon of many missed tumours in breast cancer screening. But what do we find if we re-examine the radiographs of women where the radiologist failed to catch these interval breast cancers? And what about an expert review in a legal setting?

3.10 Review after the Fact: Do not Forget to Blind!

Does it make a difference whether radiophotographs are reviewed, like in case 2, with outcome knowledge or blinded when they are examined as if they were 'new' with

46 D.D. Woods *et al.*, *Behind human error*, Ashgate Publishing Ltd 2011, pp. 235-236.

47 M.J. van Wert, T.S. Horowitz & J.M. Wolfe, 'Even in correctable search, some types of rare targets are frequently missed', *Attention, Perception, & Psychophysics* 2009, Vol. 71(3), pp. 541-553.

no additional outcome information? Empirical studies have shown that it makes all the difference! It has been demonstrated in several experiments that when mammography's of women with interval carcinomas are re-examined with blinding for the actual outcome, most are again reported as 'normal' whereas looking again at them with outcome knowledge many more abnormalities are reported.[48]

Another experiment has revealed that lesions, which may be found on radiographs in hindsight with unblended meticulous re-examination are intrinsically undetectable using eye-tracking experiments in the blinded situation. When those photos are examined 'freshly' the following of the eye movements precise registration of those movements reveal that radiologists do not spot them, they are intrinsically undetectable.[49]

These empirical studies demonstrate that in a legal context, blinded re-examination of radiographs is obligatory, for which a proper protocol should be designed. In clinical pathology a protocol for the re-examination of slides was described for an objective expert review.[50]

So, when looking at this case from different perspectives a more detailed and objective verdict on the screening radiologists's behaviour would emerge that would differ essentially from the court's original verdict of negligence.

3.11 CONCLUSION

In this chapter we have pondered on the many ways we can go astray in legal fact-finding and judgment. Both cases, the trial of the poor tram driver and the case of the unlucky woman, have shown that there is more to tort law than just the strict and sage application of the five elements of negligence.

Especially the second case has shown the statement 'context is everything' to be very true. The insights from social psychology have clearly unmasked the potential motivated biases by the plaintiff. Cognitive psychology has unravelled pitfalls when searching and interpreting facts and the final step of decision making. Finally, empirical research of the particular medical domain gives us practical information per-

48 S. Hofvind *et al.*, 'Influence of review design on percentages of missed interval breast cancers: retrospective study of interval cancers in a population-based screening program', *Radiology* 2005, Vol. 237, pp. 436-444.
49 C.F. Nodine *et al.*, 'Blinded review of retrospectively visible unreported breast cancers: an eye-position analysis', *Radiology* 2001, Vol. 221, pp. 122-129.
50 R.W.M. Giard, 'When is the practice of pathology malpractice?', *J Clin Pathol.* 2010, Vol. 63(11), pp. 957-961.

taining to the legal problem. Managing the quality of our legal endeavours requests that we step back, reflect, examine, experiment and consult other disciplines. The catchword, as was stated in the first chapter, is methodology. This methodology is always interdisciplinary in nature but the legal scholarship will remain the foundation of practicing law.

4 Groups as Motivated Information Processors: Implications for Decision Making among Judges

Femke S. Ten Velden and Carsten K.W. De Dreu

4.1 Introduction

Legal formalism is based on the premise that judges base their decisions and rulings on cases by applying the governing law in a logical, mechanical, and deliberate manner.[1] The realist movement, in contrast, is based on the premise that judges follow an intuitive process to reach consensus. Realists argue that the rational application of legal reasons does not sufficiently explain judicial decisions and that psychological, political, and social factors influence rulings as well.[2]

Just as all human beings, judges are limited in their cognitive capacity, and therefore make use of mental shortcuts (*i.e.* heuristics), and fall prey to decision biases. For example, judges sometimes use irrelevant anchor information when ruling, succumb to the hindsight bias,[3] make use of the representativeness heuristic, and are susceptible to framing.[4] Furthermore, a recent study showed that judges' favourable parole rulings dropped from 65% right after a food break to nearly 0% right before a food break.[5] All in all, these results speak to the realists' view of judges. It is not surprising therefore that recently, scholars have begun to integrate the two disparate views, and increasingly judges are seen as decision makers who sometimes rule based on instinct, and sometimes based on deliberation.[6]

1 *See* B. Neuborne, 'Of Sausage Factories and Syllogism Machines: Formalism, Realism, and Exclusionary Selection Techniques', *New York University Law Review* 1992, Vol. 67, pp. 419-449.
2 *See* J. Frank, *Law and the Modern Mind*, New York: Coward-McCann 1930.
3 The hindsight bias refers to a tendency to overestimate the predictability of past events; *see, e.g.*, S.J. LaBine & G. LaBine, 'Determination of Negligence and the Hindsight Bias', *Law and Human Behavior* 1996, Vol. 20, p. 501.
4 *See, e.g.*, J.J. Rachlinski, 'Gains, Losses, and the Psychology of Litigation', *Southern California Law Review* 1996, Vol. 70, pp. 113-85.
5 *See* S. Danziger, J. Levav & L. Avnaim-Pesso, 'Extraneous factors in judicial decisions', *Proceedings of the National Academy of Sciences* 2011, Vol. 108, pp. 6889-6892.
6 *See* C. Guthrie, J.J. Rachlinski, & A.J. Wistrich, 'Blinking on the bench: How judges decide cases', *Cornell Law Review* 2007, Vol. 93, pp. 1-44.

It is not the goal of this chapter to attempt to settle the debate of the judge as a mechanical and deliberate versus an intuitive and inherently flawed decision maker. Instead, we will provide an overview of factors that might attenuate or amplify biased judicial decision making. Put differently, we will specify under which circumstances judges' rulings are more or less likely to be influenced by something other than the governing law. More specifically, we will address theory and research that apply to situations in which judges handle cases and rule in groups, rather than in isolation, the so called multi-judge panels.

Multi-judge panels, consisting of at least three judges, are an important component of the Dutch legal system and generally rule on more complex cases, whereas less complicated cases are referred to a single judge. Multi-judge panels also play an important role in judges' education.[7] With these panels handling a substantive proportion of all legal cases, it is important for judges and policymakers alike to understand and stimulate the effective use of this system. After all, the basic premise for the inclusion of multiple judge panels into the Dutch judiciary system is that having more people equates to more knowledge, skills, and experience which can potentially positively affect the quality of decisions that are being made.

The process of decision making in multi-judge courts can be understood as a specific form of group decision making and thus differs in a number of key elements from pure individual decision making. Partly because of the private nature and confidentiality of the panel, little is known about how judgments within the panel are established. In contrast to the limited knowledge about the functioning of multi-judge panels, there is well developed literature on the role of (social) psychological factors that influence individual and group decision making. This literature is largely grounded in a long tradition of experimental laboratory research into how individuals and small groups (3-6 individuals) reach decisions. The research on individual decision making focuses primarily on cognitive and personality factors involved in decision making. The literature on group decision making describes how groups that are together for a shorter or longer time arrive at joint decisions, reach creative solutions, negotiate mutual differences, and so on. Recently scholars have begun to summarize this literature and theoretically anchored it. As a result, several factors which play an important role in individual and group decision making were identified. In this chapter, we will not address the factors that play a role in individual decisions, but rather focus on the psychological differences between individual and group decision making, and the consequences of these differences for the process and quality of decisions. Put differently, we will focus on what happens when the judging organ

7 *See* B.M. Dijksterhuis, M.J.G. Jacobs & W.M. De Jongste, *De competentiegrens van enkelvoudige kamers in strafzaken*, Den Haag: Boom Juridische Uitgevers 2003.

is not an isolated individual, but a group of people. In particular, in the following we will utilize the recently developed *Motivated Information Processing in Groups Model*[8] to describe specific characteristics of decision making groups and their impact on decision making processes and thereby the quality of the decisions.

4.2 GROUPS AS INFORMATION PROCESSORS

Groups are often assumed to be better decision makers than individuals.[9] From a (social) psychological perspective the benefits of choosing groups, as opposed to individuals, as decision makers apply when the decision is expected to be complex, and requires multiple perspectives and angles through which the information pertaining to the decision should be approached. The presence of multiple individuals in a group can create an environment in which, if used correctly, different skills and diverse knowledge lead to high quality decisions. Furthermore, the potential capacity for the storage and handling of information is greater in groups than in individuals. This idea lies at the root of multi-judge panels. Multiple judges could potentially process and integrate more information, which would increase the likelihood of reaching a high quality decision.[10] However, unlike an individual judge, multi-judge panels must work towards a consensus in order to reach decisions and produce a collective ruling, which increases the complexity and demands of the task of reaching a decision.

Past research comparing individual and group decision making has indeed shown support for the premise that groups have the potential to reach decisions of higher quality than individuals, and has identified the circumstances in which this is more likely to occur. Several review articles have compared individual and group performance on various tasks. The general consensus is that, on average, groups outperform individuals on intellective tasks, that is, tasks with clear, objective criteria for assessing the quality of performance.[11] Although groups often fail to perform as well as their best performing member, research has shown that, for example, groups may

8 For a thorough review of the model, *see* C.K.W. De Dreu, B.A. Nijstad & D. Van Knippenberg, 'Motivated information processing in group judgement and decision making', *Personality and Social Psychology Review* 2008, Vol. 12, pp. 22-49.

9 *See* C.R. Sunstein, 'Group judgments: Deliberation, statistical means, and information markets', *New York University Law Review* 2005, Vol. 80, pp. 962-1049.

10 *See, e.g.,* G.J.M. Corstens, 'De alleensprekende rechter', *NJ*, 1999, Vol. 9, pp. 392-393; J. Hartwick, B.H. Sheppard & J.H. Davis, 'Group remembering: Research and implications', *in*: R. Guzzo (Ed.), *Improving group decision-making in organizations: Approaches from theory and research*, New York: Academic Press 1982, pp. 41-72.

11 *See e.g.,* R. Hastie, S.D. Penrod & N. Pennington, *Inside the jury*, Cambridge: Harvard University Press 1986. *See* P.R. Laughlin & A.L. Ellis, 'Demonstrability and social combination processes on mathematical intellective tasks', *Journal of Experimental Social Psychology* 1986, Vol. 22, pp. 173-189.

reach an understanding or solve a problem that none of their members could have done alone.[12] Furthermore, sometimes group members develop stronger motivation and perform better in the presence of other group members than they would have done in pure isolation.[13] However, many of the tasks that groups have to perform are not unambiguously intellective. For example, rulings in legal cases can be considered intermediate between intellective and judgmental decision making tasks, with some aspects being intellective, and some aspects being judgmental. This ambiguity of many different types of group tasks makes it difficult to objectively specify a correct decision.[14] Consequently, despite the earlier mentioned positive findings, group decisions are often suboptimal either from the perspective of external parties, by a normative standard, or in the eyes of group members themselves.[15] Indeed, groups often suffer process losses, search for and discuss information in a confirmatory rather than diagnostic manner, and underestimate their own vulnerability and fallibility.[16]

Prior research has identified several reasons why group performance is sometimes suboptimal. When decisions are made in a group rather than by an individual, several aspects of the task are altered, which contributes to a broadening of task demands.[17] For example, in the group context, members are often concerned with maintaining or improving interpersonal relationships as well as making a collective judgment. Similarly, group members are likely to be concerned about the impression they make on their fellow group members and/or an external audience as they participate and contribute (or fail to do so) to the collective task. As work on groupthink[18] indicates, an excessive emphasis on reaching consensus by avoiding disagreements and conflict

12 *See e.g.*, S.N. Fraidin, 'When is one head better than two? Interdependent information in group decision making', *Organizational Behavior and Human Decision Processes* 2004, Vol. 93, pp. 102-113; P.R. Laughlin *et al.*, 'Groups perform better than the best individuals on letters-to-numbers problems: Effects of group size', *Journal of Personality and Social Psychology* 2006, Vol. 90, pp. 644-651.

13 *See* G. Hertel, N.L. Kerr & L.A. Messé, 'Motivation gains in performance groups: Paradigmatic and theoretical developments on the Kohler effect', *Journal of Personality and Social Psychology* 2000, Vol. 79, pp. 580-601; R.S. Tindale & J.R. Larson, 'Assembly bonus effect or typical group performance? A comment of Michaelsen, Watson, and Black', *Journal of Applied Psychology* 1992, Vol. 77, pp. 102-105.

14 Laughlin & Ellis 1986.

15 *See* N.L. Kerr & R.S. Tindale, 'Group performance and decision making', *Annual Review of Psychology* 2003, Vol. 55, pp. 2201-2232; B.A. Nijstad, *Group performance*, (2nd edn.), New York: Psychology Press 2009.

16 *See* I. Steiner, *Group process and productivity*, New York: Academic Press 1972; I.L. Janis & L. Mann, *Decision making: A psychological analysis of conflict, choice and commitment*, New York: Free Press 1977; S. Schulz-Hardt *et al.*, 'Biased information search in group decision making', *Journal of Personality and Social Psychology* 2000, Vol. 78, pp. 655-669.

17 *See* N.L. Kerr, R.J. MacCoun & G.P. Kramer, 'When are N heads better (or worse) than one?: Biased judgment in individuals and groups', *in*: J.H. Davis & E.H. Witte (Eds.), *Understanding group behavior: Consensual action by small groups*, Vol. 1, 1996, pp. 105-136.

18 I. Janis, *Groupthink*, (2nd edn.), Boston: Houghton-Mifflin 1982.

can interfere with thorough, accurate judgment in groups. Furthermore, the mere presence of other group members can create distractions that inhibit attentional processes, lead to a motivational loss to contribute to the group discussion due to lower identifiability of individual contributions towards the group product, or due to the possibility that other group members might compensate for information that one has missed.[19] In addition, work on idea generation has shown that groups suffer from production blocking, such that when other group members are talking, the production of one's own ideas is blocked. Production blocking thus happens when people need to take turns in expressing their opinions and exchanging their information, which is the case in groups.[20] All in all, there are several reasons why groups sometimes perform less than their potential. In order to counteract these deficiencies, it is essential to consider the ways in which groups handle, exchange, and process information that becomes available before, or during group discussion.

4.2.1 Group Level Information Processing

Recently, scholars have begun to view groups as information sharing and processing entities.[21] According to this perspective, groups, much like individuals, process information to reach decisions – individual members of a group read files, listen to interviews and statements, speak (in)formally with colleagues about a specific case, and share the information that consequently comes to the table with other members of the group. This view of groups as information processors extends earlier developments in cognitive psychology to research on group judgment and decision making. At the group level, information processing involves 'the degree to which information, ideas, or cognitive processes are shared, and are being shared, among the group members'.[22] The processing of information in groups thus involves activities that occur within as well as among the minds of individual group members. In other words, in groups, individual members search and process information, and this individual-level information processing becomes integrated with the communication and interaction between group members, thus reflecting group-level information processing.[23]

19 *See* B. Latane, K.D. Williams & S.G. Harkins, 'Many hands make light the work: The causes and consequences of social loafing', *Journal of Personality and Social Psychology* 1979, Vol. 37, pp. 823-832.

20 *See* B.A. Nijstad, W. Stroebe & H.F.M. Lodewijkx, 'Production blocking and idea generation: Does blocking interfere with cognitive processes?', *Journal of Experimental Social Psychology* 2003, Vol. 39, pp. 531–548.

21 *See, e.g.*, V.B. Hinsz, R.S. Tindale & D.A. Vollrath, 'The emerging conceptualization of groups as information processors', *Psychological Bulletin* 1997, Vol. 121, pp. 43-64.

22 Hinsz *et al.* 1997, p. 43.

23 D. Van Knippenberg, C.K.W. De Dreu & A.C. Homan, 'Work group diversity and group performance: An integrative model and research agenda', *Journal of Applied Psychology* 2004, Vol. 89, pp. 1008-1022.

As group members may differ in the information they possess, in the ideas that are most accessible, and in their preferences for certain decision alternatives, an important aspect of group judgment and decision making is how group members combine these various resources and preferences to come up with a decision. Through communication, group members can develop new insights, reach a shared understanding of the task, resolve interpersonal differences, and come up with a high-quality solution.

Despite the fact that on a conceptual level individual information processing can be translated to group level information processing, there are several notable differences. At the individual level, all available information needs to be perceived, evaluated and interpreted, to be subsequently stored in memory and retrieved when called for. In group contexts, several aspects of information processing are modified. For example, as explained earlier, attention processes might be altered due to the distractions of other group members, and as such, information might be perceived differently. Furthermore, the reactions of other group members may also affect how one evaluates and interprets available information; for example, by priming a schema or stereotype. Obviously, the potential capacity for storage and retrieval of information is greater in groups than in individuals,[24] but unfortunately, due to the above mentioned processes, this capacity is often used suboptimally.

In addition to problems occurring throughout the retrieval and processing of information stage, deficiencies can easily arise during the information sharing stage. First, individual members might not read the entire file, might pay closer attention to certain pieces of information in a file, or they might be temporarily distracted during an interview or a statement. Consequently, not all group members possess the same information. Second, when sharing information with other group members certain information might be assumed to be already known and therefore deemed unnecessary to mention. Third, the summary of facts that is often provided to group members prior to the meeting might be ambiguous, important information may have been omitted, or information might be unintentionally or intentionally accentuated. A consequence of these deficiencies is that during group discussion, certain parts of the available information will receive more attention than other parts. This can thereby create a situation in which the assumptions that arise based on the discussed information are actually a suboptimal reflection of the total information that is available to the group members. As a result, this can lead to a different final group judgment than would be the case if all information was shared and processed. Put differently, to utilize the unique knowledge, skills, and information of the different group members it is essential that all information gets shared and processed. The

24 *Cf.* Hartwick *et al.* 1982.

subsequent quality of the group's decision or judgment is thus largely dependent on the degree to which individual members share their individual knowledge and information, make it available to all group members, and process it adequately.

4.2.2 Motivated Information Processing in Groups Model

An important element to the interpretation of groups as information processors is the fact that people can, and will, choose between a shallow and heuristic versus a deep and deliberate information search-and-processing strategy. The recently developed Motivated Information Processing in Groups (MIP-G) model[25] assumes that individuals may evaluate new information, and make judgments through a quick, effortless, and heuristic processing of information that rests on well-learned prior associations. Alternatively, individuals may engage in more effortful, deliberate, and systematic processing.[26] Whereas the use of decision heuristics may sometimes help groups make satisfactory and relatively quick decisions, relying on generalized and simplified strategies may also produce disastrous decisions. Thus, deep and deliberate information search and processing may help groups prevent this from happening and can lead to high-quality decision making.[27]

4.2.2.1 Motivated Information Sharing: Hidden Profile Situations

The importance of deep and deliberate information search and processing can most clearly be gleaned from research on so-called hidden-profile situations.[28] As stated before, group members may differ in the information they possess. For example, in multi-judge panels, some judges might have read the complete file on a criminal case, while others have read a summary. Due to attention processes, some judges might have missed certain parts of a verbal statement, while others were attentive to the entire statement, and so forth. What is important here is that the assumption that when group members receive the same information, they encode and interpret this information in the same way, might be erroneous. As a result, some information in a group might be shared, and thus available to all members, while other information is

25 *See* De Dreu *et al.* 2008.

26 *See* S. Chaiken, 'The heuristic model of persuasion', *in*: M.P. Zanna, J M. Olson & C.P. Herman (Eds.), *Social influence: The Ontario symposium*, Vol. 5, 1987, pp. 3-39 ; R.E. Petty & J.T. Cacioppo, 'The elaboration likelihood model of persuasion', *in*: L. Berkowitz (Ed.), *Advances in experimental social psychology* 1986, Vol. 19, pp. 123-205.

27 *See* C.K.W. De Dreu & P.J.D. Carnevale, 'Motivational bases for information processing and strategic choice in conflict and negotiation', *in*: M.P. Zanna (Ed.), *Advances in experimental social psychology* 2003, Vol. 35, pp. 235-291; Janis 1977.

28 G. Stasser & W. Titus, 'Pooling of unshared information in group decision making: Biased information sampling during discussion', *Journal of Personality and Social Psychology* 1985, Vol. 48, pp. 1467-1478.

unshared, and unique to one or more individuals. This is the basic premise of the so called hidden profile paradigm.

In a hidden profile, group members need to decide between options (*e.g.*, the guilt or innocence of a crime suspect) and each member has two types of information pertaining to the options available: Information that is available to all group members (*i.e.* shared information) and information that is known to only some group members (unshared information). The information is distributed among members as a hidden profile, such that information supporting the best alternative is largely unshared. Thus, based on the shared information available to all group members, a suboptimal decision alternative (*e.g.*, guilty of the suspected crime) appears to be the best. However, when shared and unshared information is pooled, an alternative option (*e.g.*, innocent of the suspected crime) emerges as a superior decision alternative. Thus, by exchanging and processing unshared information, groups can make decisions of superior quality.[29]

A long tradition of research using hidden profile tasks, including more than 25 studies, shows consistent effects. First of all, group members tend to talk primarily about shared information, and attribute great weight to this information. Second, they are strongly inclined to ignore unshared information by not mentioning it, or by not taking it seriously.[30] As ideas, opinions, or information that are shared amongst most or all of the group members thus exert a disproportionate influence on the group discussion and outcome, the consequence of this phenomenon is that, in the above mentioned example, the information pertaining to the guilt of the crime suspect disproportionately influences the group discussion and decision.

4.2.3 Synopsis

The above described research highlights the importance of a thorough *exchange* of information, and the ease with which errors might occur. In search of possible remedies in the remainder of this chapter we will argue that another critical ingredient to optimal group decision making is the extent to which group members actively and systematically *process* the information that is exchanged. We will argue that during the processing and sharing of information in a group context two factors are essential. First of all, group members need to have a collective and cooperative interest, aimed at reaching consensus as well as a high quality decision or judgment. When group members are driven by collective rather than individual interests, they are more inclined to trust each other, and each other's judgments, and also pay more

29 *See* G. Stasser & Z. Birchmeier, 'Group creativity and collective choice', *in*: P.B. Paulus & B.A. Nijstad (Eds.), *Group creativity: Innovation through collaboration*, 2003, pp. 85-109.

30 *See* Stasser & Titus 1985.

attention to other group members' information and viewpoints. In reality however it appears this is not always the case, because individual group members can be driven by personal interests, such as creating a certain status in the group, or trying to impress fellow group members. We will discuss factors that influence the formation of an individual versus collective goal, and their effect on group decision making, in the next section.

Second, group members can, and will, use one of two different, mutually exclusive information processing strategies: Individuals can process information in a quick, shallow way, or they can process information in a deep, elaborate and systematic way in which all alternatives are thoroughly evaluated. When information is processed in a quick and shallow manner, it is often assessed on the basis of heuristics and prior learned associations. An example of such a heuristic, among others, is the 'consensus implies correctness' heuristic, in which case a correlation between the degree to which group members experience consensus and the correctness of a judgment is assumed: When more individuals agree, it is assumed that the chance of that judgment being the correct one is higher. This heuristic plays an important role in group decision making when there are different opinions present, and multiple individuals share an opinion while a minority has a dissenting opinion. Furthermore, individuals that process information in a shallow way show a greater tendency for stereotyping, and are more strongly affected by the way in which information is presented, rather than the actual content of the information. We will discuss factors that help, or hinder, the thorough processing of information in paragraph 4.4.

4.3 PERSONAL VERSUS COLLABORATIVE GOAL: THE ROLE OF SOCIAL MOTIVATION

Most of the work from the perspective of groups as information processors mentioned in the previous sections is done on the basis of the implicit, or explicit, assumption that group members share the common goal of reaching consensus on a high-quality decision and that no other goals, including a desire to impress or outperform one's fellow group members, exist. However, the reality of most decision making groups is different. Although some groups have members whose only goal is to reach consensus on high-quality decisions, often members are also motivated by other incentives. Individuals within groups may be driven by personal motives, including the desire to attain and maintain a high-status position within the group, to impress others by taking credit for group successes and ideas,[31] or to prove competence. Put differently, individuals in decision making groups face a mixture of cooperative incentives to

31 W. Stroebe, M. Diehl & G. Abakoumkin, 'The illusion of group effectivity', *Personality and Social Psychology Bulletin* 1992, Vol. 18, pp. 643-650.

reach high-quality group decisions and competitive, or selfish, incentives to satisfy a personal goal.[32]

Obviously, group decision making situations may differ in terms of the relative weight that cooperative versus competitive incentives carry, with some settings being primarily cooperative and others being primarily competitive. For example, management trainees working in groups might be inclined to focus on the competitive incentive of being considered for a job opening, while judges ruling on a case in a multi-judge panel might be primarily focused on making a correct assessment of the case and reaching consensus. However, individual judges might also be motivated to attain higher status, to impress colleagues, or to have their decision preference chosen. The important point here is thus, that even in settings that would suggest the presence of a cooperative, collective goal, this might not always be the case, and competitive or selfish motives might play a role.

As such, although two people may face the exact same mixture of cooperative and competitive incentives, one may emphasize the cooperative incentives and act in the interests of the group and the other may emphasize the competitive incentives and pursue his or her self-interests. Research on this mixed-motive aspect of many group tasks relies heavily on work on social motivation – the individual's preference for a particular outcome distribution between self and others. Social motivation affects whether people emphasize the cooperative or competitive aspects of a group task. For example, individuals with a cooperative motivation view the decision making process as a collaborative task in which fairness and harmony are essential. In contrast, when individuals adopt a competitive or selfish motive, they view the decision making process as a competitive task, in which power and personal success are important.

According to the MIP-G, social motivation affects the type of information individuals and groups search for, process, and communicate. Group members with a cooperative motivation are more likely to search for, attend to, and communicate information that is conducive to group goals, such as preserving and boosting harmony and achieving collectively endorsed decisions. Group members with a competitive motivation, in contrast, are more likely to search for, attend to, and communicate information that is conducive to personal goals, such as preserving or boosting their personal status and power position within the group. First and foremost, they will be motivated to incorporate their personal preference for a certain outcome into the decision, with less or no regard for the other group members' preferences.

---

32 J.H. Davis, P.R. Laughlin & S.S. Komorita, 'The social psychology of small groups: Cooperative and mixed-motive interaction', *Annual Review of Psychology* 1976, Vol. 27, pp. 501-541.

Social motivation can be rooted in stable, person-based individual differences, or can be (temporarily) induced by features of the situation. The left-hand side of Figure 1 summarizes the factors that are known to influence social motivation.[33] In the next sections, we will discuss these factors and describe the influence of social motivation on information processing, and communication processes in groups.

4.3.1 Person and Situation Based Factors Affecting Social Motivation

As can be seen in Figure 1, social motivation is related to several stable personality characteristics, such as individual differences in social value orientation[34] and agreeableness.[35] Social value orientation refers to an individual's preference for an outcome distribution between oneself, and others. Although a variety of social value orientations can be distinguished, including altruistic, competitive, individualistic, and cooperative,[36] most studies have relied on the more global distinction between pro-self and pro-social motivation. Pro-self motivation comprises both competitive and purely individualistic goals, and pro-social motivation comprises both cooperative and purely altruistic goals. In the case of pro-self motivation, individuals try to maximize their own outcomes and they have no (or negative) regard for the outcomes obtained by other group members. In contrast, individuals with a pro-social motivation try to maximize the group's outcome.

A large body of research has demonstrated that social value orientation affects a variety of attitudes and behaviours, such as the degree to which individuals trust others, value harmony, and joint welfare. The general conclusion from these studies is that individuals with a pro-social motive have a stronger tendency to trust others, to value harmony and joint welfare, an to make decisions that foster collective goals. Individuals with a pro-self motivation, in contrast, tend to distrust others, value power and personal achievement, and make decisions that foster personal goals.[37]

Similarly, social motivation can be rooted in the stable personality factor agreeableness. People high in agreeableness can be described as 'fundamentally altruistic, sympathetic to others, eager to help and be helped in return. By contrast, the disagreeable person is egocentric, skeptical of others' intentions, and competitive rather

33 This figure is based on De Dreu *et al.* 2008, Table 1.

34 *See e.g.*, C. McClintock, 'Social motives in settings of outcome interdependence', *in*: D. Druckman (Ed.), *Negotiations: Social psychological perspective*, 1977, pp. 49-77.

35 *See* W.K.B Hofstee, B. De Raad & L.R Goldberg, 'Integration of the Big Five and circumplex approaches to trait structure', *Journal of Personality and Social Psychology* 1992, Vol. 63, pp. 146-163.

36 *See* McClintock 1977.

37 For reviews, *see* De Dreu & Carnevale 2003; De Dreu *et al.* 2008; J.M. Weber, S. Kopelman & D.M Messick, 'A conceptual review of decision making in social dilemmas', *Personality and Social Psychology Review* 2004, Vol. 8, pp. 281-307.

than cooperative'.[38] Thus, an individual's level of agreeableness affects whether individuals adopt a goal aimed at collaboration or, instead, a goal aimed at achieving one's personal interests. Indeed, people scoring high on agreeableness have been shown to be cooperative and empathic,[39] and they are more likely to adopt a cooperative rather than competitive or selfish motivation.[40] For example, past research has found that compared to groups in which members are less agreeable, groups with highly agreeable members behaved less competitively, and performed better as a group.[41]

In addition to the previously mentioned person-based factors, features of the situation might also influence the degree to which group members cooperatively pursue a collaborative goal or, instead, are driven by personal goals. For example, providing instructions to ensure that individuals not just consider their own interest and preferences, but also the preferences of others can positively affect group members' pro-social motivation. Conversely, providing instructions to focus on one's own preferences raises pro-self motivation, which in turn leads to the pursuit of one's personal goals, rather than the collective goal of reaching a high quality decision.[42] Furthermore, the notion of past and future interaction with the same group members is assumed to affect social motivation. For example, individuals expecting future interaction behave more cooperatively than individuals not expecting future interaction,[43] as do groups comprised of friends rather than strangers.[44]

In sum, stable personality factors have been shown to affect an individual's social motivation, which in turn affects whether individuals in a group adopt a collaborative goal aimed at reaching consensus, or a personal goal aimed at pursuing one's own interests. However, social motivation can also be induced by situational factors. Furthermore, it may change during an ongoing group task, for example when the incentive structure changes, when group members come to like or dislike their fellow group members, or when future interaction and collaboration becomes salient. In the

---

38 P.T. Costa & R.R. McCrae, *Revised NEO Personality Inventory (NEO-PIR):Professional Manual*, 1992, p. 15, Psychological Assessment Resources, Inc.

39 *See* G.J. Feist, 'A meta-analysis of personality in scientific and artistic creativity', *Personality and Social Psychology Review* 1998, Vol. 2, pp. 290-309.

40 *See* B. Barry & R.A. Friedman, 'Bargainer characteristics in distributive and integrative negotiation', *Journal of Personality and Social Psychology* 1998, Vol. 74, pp. 345-359.

41 *See* W.G Graziano, L.A. Jensen-Campbell & E.C. Hair, 'Perceiving interpersonal conflict and reacting to it: The case for agreeableness', *Journal of Personality and Social Psychology* 1997, Vol. 70, pp. 820-835.

42 *See* De Dreu *et al.* 2008.

43 *See* O. Ben-Yoav & D. Pruitt, 'Resistance to yielding and the expectation of cooperative future interaction in negotiation', *Journal of Experimental Social Psychology* 1984, Vol. 34, pp. 323-335.

44 *See* W.R. Fry, I.J. Firestone & D.L. Williams, 'Negotiation process and outcome of stranger dyads and dating couples: Do lovers lose?', *Basic and Applied Social Psychology* 1983, Vol. 4, pp. 1-16.

following section, we will discuss how the cooperative versus competitive processes associated with social motivation affect group discussion and the subsequent decision.

4.3.2 *Effects of Social Motivation on Group Decision Making*

Previous research has uncovered several mechanisms through which social motivation affects information processing during group decision making. One of these mechanisms suggests that social motivation may lead to a bias in the type of information that is shared during a group discussion. For example, group members often have a tendency to argue for their position and consequently only mention information that is consistent with that position, so-called advocacy.[45] This evidently leads to a bias in the information they share. Such a bias is particularly likely to occur when group members have a pro-self rather than a pro-social motivation. For example, when group members have a (selfish) interest in a group decision and want a certain alternative to be chosen, they may only share the information that might lead to the group deciding on that alternative and to omit information that counters that alternative.

Furthermore, our analysis of prior literature also makes predictions about the way in which information is disseminated. Growing evidence indicates that people instantly and automatically develop ownership of their ideas, arguments, and preferences because they have spent considerable energy in developing them.[46] This ownership has two possible consequences. First, people may react defensively when their preferences are questioned, disputed, or even refuted on the basis of facts and new evidence. Second, people may self-enhance the validity, and correctness of their arguments and preferences, and this may lead them to vehemently argue for their own perspective and against new counterevidence provided by other group members. In short, during group discussion group members tend to push their own preferences, make them seem even bigger than they are, and ignore or derogate information that counters the validity of their own perspective or position. It has been suggested that pro-socially motivated individuals may be less sensitive to ownership issues; they may be less inclined to construe entitlement at the individual level and instead develop feelings of group ownership.[47] If true, this would mean that pro-socially motivated group members have less of an inclination to self-enhance their own preferences.

45 *See, e.g.*, Schulz-Hardt *et al.* 2000; Stasser & Titus 1985.

46 *See* R.P. Abelson, 'Beliefs are like possessions', *Journal for the Theory of Social Behavior* 1986, Vol. 16, pp. 223-250.

47 *See* P.J.D. Carnevale, 'Property, culture, and negotiation', in: R. Kramer & D. Messick (Eds.), *Negotiation as a social process: New trends in theory and research*, 1995, pp. 309-323.

However, pro-social motivation does not constitute a panacea to all potential problems regarding information processing and information sharing, and sometimes a pro-social motivation may lead to a bias in information sharing. Evidence for this notion can be found in several studies using the hidden profile paradigm which show that information that is held in common by all group members tends to be valued and discussed at the expense of the unique, unshared information that is held by the individual group members. Interestingly, this prior work implicitly or explicitly assumed that group members work cooperatively towards achieving the collaborative goal of reaching consensus in a high quality decision. As such, the studies discussed thus far, as well as their implications, pertain to cooperative settings. Thus, it appears that in these cooperative settings, group members are biased to focus on shared information, at the expense of unshared information, which often prevents them from making high quality group decisions.

Such a bias may occur for two reasons. First, group members with a pro-social motivation value group harmony and consensus, and they may therefore refrain from sharing information that is contrary to the group's current opinion. Put differently, they may refrain from voicing dissent. This self-censoring may lead to a tendency to abstain from sharing unique (unshared) information that runs counter to the group's preference and may therefore contribute to a lower quality group decision. Furthermore, if group members decide to share information that is contrary to the group's consensus, it might become downplayed. In these situations, a high pro-social motivation may thus also lead to a bias in information sharing.

A second reason that might account for a bias in information sharing in pro-social groups is that shared information has the property that it can be validated by other group members.[48] As a consequence, group members who mention shared information are perceived to be more central to the group and more knowledgeable and competent than those who mention unshared information. Also, group members who possess a large amount of shared information are more influential. We argue that this process of mutual enhancement will occur more often in groups with a pro-social motive because pro-social group members are more likely to seek to encourage and validate each other's points of view in order to enhance cooperation and harmony. Thus, self-censoring and mutual enhancement is more likely to occur in pro-social than in pro-self groups and biases information provision and exchange towards shared rather than unshared information.

48 G.M. Wittenbaum, A.P. Hubbell & C. Zuckerman, 'Mutual enhancement: Toward an understanding of the collective preference for shared information', *Journal of Personality and Social Psychology* 1999, Vol. 77, pp. 967-978.

4.3.3 Synopsis

To summarize, according to the MIP-G model, the individual's pro-self versus pro-social motivation biases the type of information that someone looks for, generates, and processes. This notion suggests that individuals with a pro-social motivation are more likely to search, encode, and retrieve information consistent with and conducive to group rather than personal goals, and with preserving harmony. Because of their stronger focus on coordination and harmony, pro-social groups may, thus, self-censor more and value shared information more than pro-self groups. In contrast, individuals with a pro-self motivation are more likely to search, encode, and retrieve information conducive to personal goals. In pro-self groups, this may lead to advocacy (*i.e.*, only mentioning information that is consistent with one's preference). However, a pro-self orientation is associated with greater independent thinking, which may actually result in a higher valuation of unique, unshared information, and consequently the attainment of higher quality group decisions. On the other hand, it may also reduce attention to others' ideas and information, or even lead to derogation and criticism of this information.

Thus, work on social motivation presents an interesting conundrum. One the one hand it appears that the more members have or adopt a pro-self motivation, the less likely it is that the group focuses on consensus and integration of perspectives, emphasizes the value of shared information, and tolerates dissent and independence. This may promote the exchange of unique, unshared information, which is essential to arriving at a high quality decision. However, on the other hand, the more members have a pro-self motivation, the less likely it is that others' ideas and information are considered and integrated into one's own thinking and decision making. It can thus be inferred that groups with pro-socially motivated members may be better at reaching decisions that include all group members' preferences, but may be worse at reaching decisions when members hold unique information that might lead to a deviation from the dominant preference in the group.

This paradox is well illustrated in research studying the effects of member familiarity on the quality of the group decision. As mentioned previously, group members that are familiar with each other behave more cooperatively during group discussion and more often pursue a cooperative goal during decision making, than group members that are unfamiliar with each other. One study found that groups composed of friends solved a hidden profile better than groups composed of strangers.[49] Other studies

49 *See* D.H. Gruenfeld *et al.*, 'Group composition and decision making: How member familiarity and information distribution affect process and performance', *Organizational Behavior and Human Decision Processes* 1996, Vol. 67, pp. 1-15.

found quite the opposite effect: groups composed of members with an established relationship mentioned less unshared information than ad hoc groups of strangers.[50] Furthermore, when group members know each other's preferences, a situation that is more likely to occur when group members are familiar with each other, they pay less attention to each other's arguments, which negatively affects the quality of the group decision.[51] Thus, it appears that both pro-self and pro-socially motivated groups are vulnerable to biases in information process and exchange.

As evidenced by the research discussed above, having groups discuss and decide co-operatively, with a collaborative goal aimed at achieving consensus and harmony might not be sufficient. Pro-social groups need to overcome their tendency toward self-censoring and overvaluing shared information, and incorporate individual members' unique information by exchanging (unshared) information and process this information. In the following, we propose that in addition to a cooperative goal of reaching consensus, groups need to process information in a thorough, deliberate way.

4.4 THE DEPTH OF INFORMATION PROCESSING: EPISTEMIC MOTIVATION

As stated previously, the way in which group members evaluate, share, and integrate information that becomes available during the group discussion determines the quality of the subsequent decision or judgment. According to the Motivated Information Processing in Groups Model (MIP-G),[52] the extent to which information is processed systematically depends on group members' epistemic motivation – *i.e.* their willingness to expend effort to achieve a thorough and rich understanding of the world, including the group task or judgment decision at hand.

Heuristic processing of information is more likely to occur with low levels of epistemic motivation, whereas deep and deliberate processing is more likely with high levels of epistemic motivation. Epistemic motivation depends on the perceived sufficiency of the information that is already available to the decision maker, which has been termed the sufficiency principle.[53] The more decision makers perceive their cur-

50 *See, e.g.*, B.E Mennecke & J.S. Valacich, 'Information is what you make of it: The influence of group history and computer support on information sharing, decision quality, and member perceptions', *Journal of Management Information Systems* 1998, Vol. 15, pp. 173-197.

51 *See* A. Mojzisch & S. Schulz-Hardt, 'Knowing others' preferences degrades the quality of group decisions', *Journal of Personality and Social Psychology* 2010, Vol. 98, pp. 794-808.

52 *See* De Dreu *et al.* 2008.

53 *See* S. Chaiken, A. Liberman & A.H. Eagly, 'Heuristic and systematic information processing within and beyond the persuasion context', *in*: J.S. Uleman & J.A. Bargh (Eds.), *Unintended thought*, 1989, pp. 212-252; S. Chaiken & Y. Trope (Eds.), *Dual-process theories in social psychology*, New York: Guilford 1999.

rent state of knowledge and information as insufficient to make a decision of satisfactory quality, the more they are motivated to engage in systematic processing of decision-relevant information. In contrast, when decision makers feel they already have sufficient information to make a decision, epistemic needs are satisfied and there will be no additional search for and processing of new information.

Epistemic motivation can be rooted in stable, person-based individual differences, or can be (temporarily) induced by features of the situation. Figure 1 presents an overview of several person and situational factors that induce, or reduce, epistemic motivation. In the next section, we will describe this is more detail.

Figure 1: Examples of Person and Situation Antecedents to Social Motivation and to Epistemic Motivation

	Prosocial Motivation	Epistemic Motivation
Person based	Pro-social value orientation (+) Agreeableness (+) Disposition to trust (+)	Need for cognition (+) Need for structure (–) Need for Cognitive closure (–) Openness to experience (+)
Situation based	Cultural collectivism (+) Cooperative reward system (+) Third-party instructions to cooperate (+) Pro-social norms, climate (+) Collective identity (+) Anticipated future interaction (+) Past cooperation (+)	Accountability to process (+) Time pressure (–) Power preponderance (–) External threat (–) Preference diversity (+) Strong minorities (+) Autocratic leadership (–)

NOTE: (+), (–) indicate more or less of that particular motivation, respectively; the list is nonexhaustive and reflects empirically well-established antecedents.

4.4.1 Person Based Factors Affecting Epistemic Motivation

4.4.1.1 Need for Cognitive Closure

As can be seen in Figure 1, epistemic motivation is inversely related to the Need for Cognitive Closure, a stable personality factor that refers to the individual's desire for a firm, unambiguous answer. Individuals at the high need for closure end of the continuum are characterized by cognitive impatience, they leap to judgment on the basis of inconclusive evidence and they display rigidity of thought. At the other end of the continuum, individuals with low need for closure may prefer to suspend judgment, engage in extensive information search and generate multiple interpretations for known facts. Compared to individuals with low need for closure, individuals high in need for closure are more strongly affected by initial impressions, rely more on existing stereotypic knowledge, and react more negatively to people opposing group consensus. [54]

Indeed, research has shown that Need for Cognitive Closure affects the degree to which people react to and are influenced by early or pre-existing cues. For example, due to limited cognitive ability, humans have a tendency to base estimates on irrelevant anchor information, and adjust their estimates inappropriately.[55] This anchoring bias – the tendency to overly rely on an arbitrary chosen reference point, has been shown to occur more when individuals have a high need for closure than when individuals have a low need for closure. Individuals with high need for closure tend to seize information quickly, thus coming to quick (rather than rich, well-developed, and accurate) conclusions and subsequently freeze on those conclusions. Thus, once closure is reached they tend to stick to them.[56] In contrast, individuals with low need for closure postpone judgment until they have processed as much information as possible. Thus, a high need for cognitive closure is similar to low epistemic motivation, particularly after an initial opinion or conclusion has been reached.

4.4.1.2 Need for Cognition

Similarly, Need for Cognition refers to the way individuals regard their surroundings and the problems that arise, and think about the decisions that need to be made. Individuals with a high Need for Cognition are characterized by a strong intrinsic need to process information in a thorough, intensive way. They thoroughly study and use available information, are more attentive to the quality of the arguments in a persuasive communication, are less likely than individuals with low need for cognition to be influenced by peripheral cues such as the attractiveness of a communicator, and search for more information when they perceive the available information to be insufficient. In a study concerning dyadic decision making, members with high need for cognition were viewed by their discussion partners as being more effective persuaders, and as generating more valid arguments than their low need for cognition counterparts. In contrast, individuals with a low Need for Cognition are more inclined to trust the judgment and knowledge of others, and more often base their own judgment on heuristics.[57] For example, research using mock juries found that jury members with a high need for cognition were more active during deliberation,

54 For an extensive review, *see* A.W. Kruglanski & D.M. Webster, 'Motivated closing of the mind: "Seizing" and "freezing"', *Psychological Review* 1996, 103, pp. 263-283.

55 *See* A. Tversky & D. Kahneman, 'Judgment under Uncertainty: Heuristics and Biases', *Science* 1974, Vol. 185, pp. 1124-1131.

56 *See* Kruglanski & Webster 1996.

57 *See* D. Shestowsky, D.T Wegener & L.R. Fabrigar, 'Need for cognition and interpersonal influence: Individual differences in impact on dyadic decisions', *Journal of Personality and Social Psychology* 1998, Vol. 74, pp. 1317-1328.

spoke longer, used more persuasive arguments and were less likely to be convinced by their fellow jury members than individuals with a low need for cognition.[58]

4.4.1.3 Need for Structure

Finally, Need for Structure, the tendency to use generalized simplified representations of previous experiences to reduce the use of cognitive resources, has been shown to influence the depth of information processing. Individuals with a high Need for Structure are characterized by a chronic preference for simplicity and structure; they view the world and the decision to be made in less complex ways, and often rely on a shallow, heuristic processing of information. In contrast, individuals with a low Need for Structure are characterized by a preference for complexity and spontaneity, are less likely to rely on heuristics, and are more likely to incorporate new information into their decision making process.[59] Research has shown that individuals with a high need for structure more often rely on stereotypic cues, and simplify the problem at hand.[60] More recent studies have further shown that individuals with a high need for structure are less tolerant to dissenting (minority) viewpoints, which they are inclined to ignore or even actively oppress.[61] In short, those with low need for structure are more likely to display high epistemic motivation, which means they are less likely to rely on heuristics and more likely to incorporate new information into their decision making process.

The degree to which individuals in a group exchange information, and process this information in either a shallow, heuristic way or a more thorough, deliberate way depends strongly, in addition to the abovementioned person based factors, on a large number of situation-based factors. For example, individuals' need to make a decision quickly, and thus their epistemic motivation, might change during the course of group discussion, for instance due to increased time pressure. In the following, we will elaborate on those factors that are relevant within the context of judicial decision making in full bench panels.

58 *See* D. Shestowsky & L.M Horowitz, 'How the Need for Cognition scale predicts behavior in mock jury deliberations', *Law and Human Behavior* 2004, Vol. 28, pp. 305-337.

59 *See* S.L. Neuberg & J. Newsom, 'Personal need for structure: Individual differences in the desire for simple structure', *Journal of Personality and Social Psychology* 1993, Vol. 65, pp. 113-131.

60 *See* M.M Thompson *et al.*, 'The personal need for structure and personal fear of invalidity measures: Historical perspectives, current applications, and future directions', *in*: G.B. Moskowitz (Ed.), *Cognitive social psychology: The Princeton symposium on the legacy and future of social cognition*, 2001, pp. 19-39.

61 *See* A.W Kruglanski *et al.*, 'Groups as epistemic providers: Need for closure and the unfolding of group centrism', *Psychological Review* 2006, Vol. 113, pp. 84-100.

4.4.2 *Situation Based Factors Affecting Epistemic Motivation*

4.4.2.1 Time Pressure

Time pressure arises when a decision deadline looms, when a case might get barred, or simply when time runs out and the next case needs to be handled. From a psychological perspective, the reasons concerning why time pressure arises are less relevant, as long as time pressure is psychologically experienced by individuals – regardless of whether it is actually present. At the individual level time pressure affects the way information is handled, and evaluated. For example, research found under time pressure, individuals simplify their information processing, and, for example, pay more attention to, and base their decision more often on specific types of information. For example, when the decision to be made involves buying a product, individuals under time pressure are more inclined to base their decision on information that speaks to the negative characteristics, thereby ignoring positive characteristics.[62] Furthermore, time pressure intensifies the tendency to seek cognitive closure, which makes individuals more likely to base their opinions on initial impressions, stereotypical cues, and anchors.[63]

A large body of research has shown that when groups experience time pressure, less information is exchanged and the quality of the decision declines.[64] In addition, when operating under time pressure, groups are less likely to revise erroneous assumptions and judgments, and groups are strongly influenced by routines and standard protocols.[65] Recent research has further demonstrated that when groups operate under time pressure, biases tend to be amplified. In a study using mock judges, three-person groups were presented with four criminal cases in which the guilt or innocence of the suspect needed to be assessed. The results of this study showed that when groups operated under time pressure, they were more likely to judge the suspect of the fourth case to be guilty when they had judged the suspects from the first three cases to be innocent, and vice versa.[66] This phenomenon is known as the Gambler's Fallacy, a pervasive decision bias that affects how people judge repeated occurrences of the same

62 *See* P. Wright, 'The Harassed Decision Maker: Time Pressures, Distractions and the Use of Evidence', *Journal of Applied Psychology* 1974, Vol. 59, pp. 555-561.

63 *See* A.W. Kruglanski & T. Freund, 'The freezing and unfreezing of lay inferences: Effects of impressional primacy, ethnic stereotyping, and numerical anchoring', *Journal of Experimental Social Psychology* 1983, Vol. 19, pp. 448-468.

64 *See* J.R. Kelly & S.J. Karau, 'Group decision making: The effects of initial preferences and time pressure', *Personality and Social Psychology Bulletin* 1999, Vol. 25, pp. 1342-1354.

65 *See* E. De Grada *et al.*, 'Motivated cognition and group interaction: Need for closure affects the contents and processes of collective negotiations', *Journal of Experimental Social Psychology* 1999, Vol. 35, pp. 346-365.

66 F.S. Ten Velden & C.K.W. De Dreu, unpublished manuscript, University of Amsterdam, 2011.

situation.[67] For example, if a coin is tossed five times, and the first four times tails come up, the gambler's fallacy causes individuals to incorrectly believe that heads is more likely to come up in the fifth toss.

In a similar study, groups operating under time pressure based their judgment regarding the guilt or innocence of a crime suspect, and the subsequent sentence, more frequently on personality information about that suspect rather than on situational information, such as opportunity.[68] This bias is known as the Fundamental Attribution Error, and refers to the tendency to over-value personality-based explanations for the observed behaviours of others while under-valuing situational explanations for those behaviours.[69] In sum, time pressure reduces epistemic motivation, so that groups switch to heuristic, shallow information processing, which leads to an increase in the occurrence of decision biases.

4.4.2.2 Process Accountability

Process accountability[70] refers to the degree individuals expect to be observed and evaluated by others.[71] Multiple studies have shown that the quality of a decision is increased when the decision to be made is deemed important and when group members are made process accountable. It has further been argued that individuals under process accountability tend to be more critical, which leads to a more thorough evaluation of decision alternatives. Indeed, individuals who were held process accountable evaluated decision alternatives more thoroughly, and relied less on heuristic cues than individuals who were not held process accountable.[72]

Recent research has further demonstrated that the effects of process accountability on systematic, deliberate and thorough information processing also positively affect the quality of a group decision.[73] Using the hidden profile task we mentioned earlier,

67 *See* Tversky & Kahneman 1974.

68 Ten Velden & De Dreu 2011.

69 For a more elaborate description of attribution errors, *see e.g.*, L. Ross, 'The intuitive psychologist and his shortcomings: Distortions in the attribution process', *Advances in Experimental Social Psychology* 1977, Vol. 10, pp. 174-221.

70 Process accountability should be distinguished from outcome accountability, which refers to the degree individuals are expected to account for the decision itself, rather than the manner in which the decision was made; *see* J.S. Lerner & P.E. Tetlock, 'Accounting for the effects of accountability', *Psychological Bulletin* 1999, Vol. 125, pp. 255-275.

71 Lerner & Tetlock 1999.

72 C.K.W De Dreu, S. Koole & W. Steinel, 'Unfixing the fixed-pie: A motivated information-processing account of integrative negotiation', *Journal of Personality and Social Psychology* 2000, Vol. 79, pp. 975-987.

73 L. Scholten *et al.*, 'Motivated information processing and group decision making: Effects of process accountability on information processing and decision quality', *Journal of Experimental Social Psychology* 2007, Vol. 33, pp. 539-552.

groups under process accountability, (a) indicated more strongly that they needed additional information in order to make a high quality decision; (b) reported greater motivation to engage in deep and systematic information processing and (c) repeated unshared information more frequently during the group discussion. Groups that used this more systematic, intensive way of information processing arrived at the correct decision alternative more often than groups that performed the task without process accountability. In sum, process accountability raises epistemic motivation, and makes groups exchange more relevant information, and process this information more thoroughly, which leads to better quality decisions.

4.4.3 Group Level Factors Affecting Epistemic Motivation

4.4.3.1 Preference Homogeneity and Criticality Norm

Besides these abovementioned situation based factors, there are several characteristics of the group that affect whether groups process information in a shallow and heuristic manner or instead, in a more intensive, systematic way. In particular, preference homogeneity within groups has been shown to lead to higher levels of confidence of group members in the correctness of their judgments and ideas. When groups experience high agreement among their members with regard to the decision that has to be made, group members will often feel sufficiently confident in their judgments, which undermines further search for information. On the other hand, preference heterogeneity (*i.e.*, group members hold, *a priori*, different rather than the same preferences) may decrease the confidence of individual members and therefore increases further information search.[74]

Similarly, when groups engage in self-critical assessment of the judgment processes, they process and exchange more relevant information. For example, having groups first perform a task in which they have to be critical induces a criticality norm, which leads to greater sharing of unshared information and better performance than when groups first performed a task aimed at reaching consensus.[75] In sum, preference homogeneity leads groups to become more confident and less critical in their assessment of the correctness of their preferences. This, in turn, leads to a reduction in epistemic motivation and decreases the thorough, systematic processing of relevant information.

74 *See, e.g.*, S. Baker & R. Petty, 'Majority and minority influence: source-position imbalance as a determinant message scrutiny', *Journal of Personality and Social Psychology* 1994, Vol. 67, pp. 5-19; S. Schulz-Hardt, M. Jochims & D. Frey, 'Productive conflict in group decision making: Genuine and contrived dissent as strategies to counteract biased information seeking', *Organizational Behavior and Human Decision Processes* 2002, Vol. 88, pp. 563-586.

75 *See* T. Postmes, R. Spears & S. Cihangir, 'Quality of decision making and group norms', *Journal of Personality and Social Psychology* 2001, Vol. 80, pp. 918-930.

4.4.3.2 Decision Rules and Minority Dissent

Moreover, in contrast to individual decision making, group decision making and judgment requires the use of a decision rule. Decision rules are formal or informal procedural agreements regarding the way a decision needs to be made. Decision rules vary in terms of the degree of consensus required to lead to the selection of an alternative. In most cases, the choice stands between two different rules: Unanimity rule or majority rule.[76] The use of unanimity rule implies that *all* members of a group have to agree in order to reach a decision. In contrast, the use of majority rule implies consensus in a majority of the group; put differently, not all members have to agree in order to reach a decision. Research into the psychological effects of the use of these rules has produced some relevant findings. For example, US juries perceive the use of unanimity rule, as compared to majority rule, as more complex, and the use of this rule leads to less decisions and longer deliberations. In addition, when using unanimity rule, group decisions are more likely to resemble the initial preference of the most extreme member, than when majority rule is used.

The results of this research suggest that the use of unanimity rule stimulates systematic, intensive information processing, and reduces the quick and shallow processing of information. One possible explanation for these findings is that when using unanimity rule, individual members' contributions to the final decision become more pronounced as each member is required to make a decision and have an opinion on the case at hand. As such, group members with different opinions might be heard more than when groups use majority rule. Although majority factions often prevail in group decision making, sometimes minority factions succeed in convincing a majority. Even if they do not succeed in actually converting the majority to adopt their position, minority dissent has been found to stimulate divergent thinking, reduce confirmatory information search, reduce group polarization, prevent groupthink, and reduce conformity[77]. The MIP-G model suggest that minority dissent can have these effects because it raises epistemic motivation and therefore causes group members to abandon decision heuristics (such as 'consensus implies correctness') and instead switch to elaborate and deep information processing. Even though systematic research into this issue is lacking, this process might occur especially when groups use unanimity rule, as opposed to majority rule, and minorities with dissenting viewpoints are able to exert influence.

76 *See* M.F. Kaplan & C.E. Miller, 'Group decision making and normative versus informational influence: Effects of type of issue and assigned decision rule', *Journal of Personality and Social Psychology* 1987, Vol. 53, pp. 306-313; Stasser & Birchmeier 2003.

77 *See* D.H. Gruenfeld, M.C. Thomas-Hunt & P.H. Kim, 'Cognitive flexibility, communication strategy, and integrative complexity in groups: Public versus private reactions to majority and minority status, *Journal of Experimental Social Psychology* 1998, Vol. 34, pp. 202-226; Schulz-Hardt *et al.* 2000.

4.4.3.3 Power and Status Differences

Individual differences between group members, such as power or status differences, have also been known to affect the processes and quality of group decisions. Power differences in groups can be caused by different factors. For example, status differences within a group based on seniority might contribute to a perceived difference in power among the members. In addition, the different roles that members have in a group might affect perceived power differences, *e.g.*, one member might have the role of chairman, or a supervisor and subordinate might be part of the same group. For example, in Dutch full bench panels, it is customary that junior judges, or judges that are in training, take up a seat. In addition, the chair position is often occupied by the most senior member of the group. As such, power differences based on seniority, knowledge, and status might easily arise, and this in turn might affect subsequent decision making.

For instance, research has shown that power differences affect the degree to which individuals search for, and process, confirming or diagnostic information. It has been argued that low power individuals (re)gain control over their situation by paying close and careful attention to their powerful other, so as to accurately predict other's needs, desires, and possible actions.[78] Indeed, individuals with less status were found to more often repeat shared information in a hidden profile task, than individuals with higher status. One possible explanation for this finding might be that repeating information that all members in a group arc familiar with might bc a tool to gain more status, as members who hold more shared information exert more influence in the group than members who hold more unshared information.[79] Furthermore, research has shown that individual judges' concern for their professional reputations affects decision making, especially their reputation *vis-à-vis* their colleagues.[80] Thus, it could be argued that less powerful group members, or group members with low status are more likely to acquiesce with the more powerful group member, and thus refrain from expressing dissenting opinions. Indeed, it has been argued that individuals with a power disadvantage are more motivated to produce and maintain a certain impression for others than individuals with a power advantage.[81] Consequently, the group decision may actually reflect the judgment of the most powerful group member rather than the integration of all group members' judgments.

78 *See* S.T. Fiske, 'Controlling other people: The impact of power on stereotyping', *American Psychologist* 1992, Vol. 48, pp. 621-628.

79 *See* G.M. Wittenbaum, 'Information sampling in decision-making groups: The impact of members' task-relevant status', *Small Group Research* 1998, Vol. 29, pp. 57-84.

80 *See* N. Garoupa & T. Ginsburg, 'Guarding the Guardians: Judicial Councils and Judicial Independence', *American Journal of Comparative Law* 2009, Vol. 57, pp. 103-134.

81 *See* J.T. Copeland, 'Prophecies of power: Motivational implications of social power for behavioral confirmation', *Journal of Personality and Social Psychology* 1994, Vol. 67, pp. 264-277.

4.4.3.4 Leadership

Finally, a group-level factor that may influence group members' epistemic motivation is the approach taken by the group leader. Specifically, some studies suggest that transformational- leadership – leadership through an inspiring vision and intellectual stimulation of followers – stimulates group members to contribute ideas to the group.[82] Other research suggests that autocratic and highly directive leadership approaches undermine the degree to which followers think independently and deliberately about their tasks.[83] In line with this reasoning, research on production blocking shows that when one person dominates group discussion, others are inhibited from sharing information and ideas.[84]

The extent to which a leader is capable of facilitating discussion and extracting relevant problem-solving information from group members will thus affect the quality of group decisions.[85] Although systematic research is scarce, it seems reasonable to assume that specific approaches by the group leader affect group-level epistemic motivation. Preliminary evidence for this idea stems from research showing that when groups operate under highly directive leaders, they exchange less information, and consequently make suboptimal decisions.[86] Thus, highly directive, authoritarian leaders appear to reduce group members' epistemic motivation.

4.4.4 Synopsis

In sum, several person based and situation based factors affect group members' shallow versus systematic information processing, which in turn affects the quality of the group's decision. We have provided an overview of these factors, and their subsequent effect on epistemic motivation. Some person-based factors were found to decrease epistemic motivation, and increase shallow, heurist processing of information, such as high Need for Closure and Structure, and low Need for Cognition. Furthermore, time pressure was found to reduce epistemic motivation, as was preference homogeneity and the presence of a highly directive leader. Fortunately, we have also identified factors that increase epistemic motivation and the concomitant systematic and deep processing of information, such as low Need for Closure and Structure, and high need for Cognition. Furthermore, process accountability increases epistemic motivation, as does the use of unanimity rule or the presence of several different opinions and preferences in a group.

---

82 *See* B.M. Bass, *Leadership and performance beyond expectations*, New York: Free Press 1985.

83 G. Yukl, *Leadership in organizations*, (6th edn.), Upper Saddle River: Prentice-Hall 2006.

84 *See* Nijstad *et al.* 2003.

85 *See* De Dreu *et al.* 2008.

86 B. Nevicka, F.S. Ten Velden, A.H.B. De Hoogh & A.E.M. Vianen, 'Reality at odds with perceptions: Narcissistic leaders and group performance', *Psychological Science* 2011, Vol. 22, pp. 1259-1264.

Taken together, research on epistemic motivation in group decision making suggests that groups benefit from a deep and deliberate processing of information. Groups exchange more unshared information, and consequently make decisions of higher quality when they are motivated to process information in a thorough, deep, and systematic way. It is important to note that as the contributions of individual members need to be combined to produce a coherent, feasible, and high quality group judgment or decision, an intensive, deliberate and systematic way of information processing will only be beneficial, and increase decision quality, when group members share information from a cooperative perspective and with a collective interest and goal. The presence of a personal or collective goal affects the degree to which group members listen to each other's arguments and information, share information with others, and as such also the quality of the decision they make. Unfortunately, as stated earlier, group members are often inclined to share only those pieces of information that are congruent with their own preference or opinion. This trend is especially salient when group members strive to achieve a personal goal and pursue their own interests, as opposed to a collective goal and interests.

Similarly, the presence of a cooperative goal aimed at collaboration and reaching consensus is necessary, but in isolation does not suffice. As evidenced by research on social motivation in group decision making, pro-social groups, compared with pro-self groups, place greater value on inclusion, harmony, and reaching the collaborative goal of consensus. Furthermore, they are less likely to use information to attain a personal goal or preference. Unfortunately, in comparison to pro-self groups, they also have a tendency to overly focus on attaining consensus, which leads to less tolerance of dissent at the expense of individual members' unique information. Therefore, pro-social group members need to be motivated to share all information, even when this information might undermine the ruling consensus. One way of overcoming this issue is to promote deep and thorough processing of information. Thus, in addition to pro-social motivation, group members need to have high epistemic motivation.

4.5 Concluding Remarks

As long as we routinely rely on multi-judge benches to rule important cases, it is important to minimize bias in group judgment. Relying on a wealth of research on individual and group decision making, and the Motivated Information Processing in Groups Model in particular, we identified factors that amplify or attenuate biased decision making in groups. The core insights that emerge from the current review are three-fold. First, groups are potentially well-equipped to rule in complex cases where facts mingle with more subjective estimates and opinions, where different expertise is useful, and where information is too abundant and complex to be processed well by a single individual. However, like individuals working alone, individuals working in groups also invoke cognitive shortcuts and decision heuristics to selectively reduce information complexity, and hence may arrive at biased judgments and conclusions. In fact, group settings in and of itself provide no antidote to biased judgment and decision making and, even worse, in cases amplify rather than reduce individual biases in information processing and judgment.

Second, group settings bring along a set of unique biases that may impact group judgments and decisions in important ways. We have discussed how lack of epistemic motivation leads group members to exchange and integrate information in rather sub-optimal ways, rendering higher the likelihood of bias judgment and erroneous decision making. Epistemic motivation resides in judges' individual traits and personalities, with lower need for cognition, and higher need for cognitive closure driving towards shallow and loose rather than deliberate and systematic information processing and exchange. Epistemic motivation is also influenced by contextual factors. Time pressure, fatigue, and autocratic leadership all reduce epistemic motivation; process accountability and being in low-power positions up-regulate epistemic motivation and concomitant deliberate information processing and exchange. Thus, through staffing decisions and in the design of multi-judge benches, practice may take into account to potentially detrimental effects on judgment quality of certain personality traits alone or in conjunction with environmental conditions like time pressure, workload, and within-group power differentials.

Third, and finally, we reviewed research showing that individuals within groups may operate on the basis of a more or less competitive versus cooperative motivation. Stronger cooperative motivation manifests itself in stronger tendencies to self-sacrifice personal interests and opinions for the benefit of others, and the overarching group. Under stronger cooperative motivation, power differentials become less important and status seeking tendencies are reduced. Also, under stronger cooperative motivation group members have greater trust in others, are less inclined to (self) censor deviating opinions, and are more inclined to share and integrate information. Importantly, there is reason to assume that these potentially beneficial effects of cooperative motivation come about especially when group members have high rather than low epistemic motivation. Under low epistemic motivation, cooperative tendencies lead group members towards quick compromises and heuristic-based consensus decisions. Only when epistemic motivation is high do cooperatively motivated group members truly benefit from the greater exchange of information, opinions, and insights.

Most of the studies reported and reviewed here were conducted using laboratory experiments with groups that came together for a relatively short period of time. This notwithstanding, we believe that the common biases uncovered and discussed here, such as the focus on shared information that is held in common by all group members at the expense of unique information that is only held by one member, pertain to decision making by multi-judge benches. In describing factors that enhance intensive, deliberate and thorough information processing in groups, we have identified several possible mechanisms through which biased decision making can be decreased. In quite a number of cases factors undermining epistemic and/or cooperative motivation are under the control of those making staffing decisions, or designing the structural context within which multi-bench judges operate. In these cases, smart thinking and informed practice may be as effective as financially costly interventions may be. We hope that our review of the processes underlying high quality group decision making not only serve as a scholarly inquiry into judicial decision making, but also provide the insights for those concerned with improving the practice of both individual and group decision making in legal contexts.

5 How Judges Make Decisions

Jeffrey J. Rachlinski

Judge Jerome Frank once remarked that 'when all is said and done, we must face the fact that judges are human'.[1] When making decisions, human beings commonly rely on simple rules of thumb, or mental shortcuts, that psychologists term 'heuristics'.[2] So too, do judges.[3] Judges' reliance on these heuristics produces intuitions about how they will decide the cases that come before them. These intuitions can be surprisingly accurate, but also often lead to errors in judgment. Judges therefore need to check this intuition carefully. Accurate judging requires that judges engage in careful, deliberative assessments.[4]

The thesis that judges have intuitive responses to cases that must be checked against deliberative assessments arises directly from the contemporary research on the psychology of judgment and choice. Several lines of research in this field have converged on the idea that human beings use two distinct systems of reasoning to make decisions: an intuitive system (often called 'system 1') and a deliberative system ('system 2').[5] System 1 consists of judgments that are intuitive, associative, affective, and rapid; system 2 consists of judgments that that are deliberative, rule-based, calculating, and slow.

Although the dual-process model of judgment and choice has gained great currency, it is imperfect. The brain contains a large number of distinct processes and uses a wide range of cognitive strategies, many of which do not fit neatly into the intuitive/deliberative distinction.[6] Furthermore, although system 2 can be best described as the rational part of the brain, system 1 is a less coherent concept. Rather than an

1 J. Frank, *Courts on Trial: Myth and Reality in American Justice*, Princeton University Press 1949, p. 410.

2 *See* A. Tversky & D. Kahneman, 'Judgment Under Uncertainty: Heuristics and Biases', *Science* 1974, Vol. 185 No. 4157, pp. 1124-1131.

3 *See* C. Guthrie, J.J. Rachlinski & A.J. Wistrich, 'Inside the Judicial Mind', *Cornell Law Review* 2001, Vol. 86, No.4, pp. 777- 830.

4 *See* C. Guthrie, J.J. Rachlinski & A.J. Wistrich, 'Blinking on the Bench: How Judges Decide Cases', *Cornell Law Review* 2007, Vol. 93, No. 1, pp. 1-44.

5 *See* D. Kahneman, *Thinking, Fast and Slow*, New York: Farrar, Straus & Giroux 2011.

6 *See* M. Lubell *et al.*, 'Institutional Design Capitalizing on the Intuitive Nature of Decision Making', *in*: C. Engel & W. Singer (Eds.), *Better than Conscious: Exploiting the Capacity of Humans to Reach Decisions by Both Serial and Parallel Processing of Information*, Cambridge, MA: MIT Press 2006, pp. 413-432.

intuitive system, system 1 might be best described as anything that is not system 2.[7] Nevertheless, this simple distinction describes a surprisingly broad array of phenomena of judgment and choice. Furthermore, system 1 processes all tend to be effortless and automatic, whereas system 2 reasoning is demanding.[8] The concept of dual-process reasoning might be best thought of as a handy metaphor than a perfectly accurate model of human judgment.

Despite its theoretical shortcomings, the dual-process model of human judgment dovetails well with a long debate between legal formalists and legal realists about judicial decision making.[9] System 1 closely resembles the model of judicial decision making that the legal realists outlined. Legal realists argued that judges have "hunches" about how they will decide a case – even before they have completely thought through the law and the facts.[10] These hunches arise from judges' socio-economic backgrounds, politics, or even their emotions.

Legal formalists, in contrast, argue that judges primarily apply rules and precedent. For formalists, judges spend their time carefully identifying relevant statutes and cases, resolving conflicts between different rules through the use of widely accepted reasoning processes, and then applying these rules to the facts before them. This view has been characterized as an assertion that judges are essentially, 'giant syllogism machines'.[11] This mechanistic view of judges is nearly identical to how psychologists describe system 2. Psychologists intend system 2 to reflect the human ability to use logical rules and reasons to make decisions. The mechanistic understanding of statutes and precedent thus mimics the formalists' understanding of what judges are doing.

Although the debate between the formalists and realist is decades old, it still resonates today. Chief Justice John Roberts of the United States Supreme Court succinctly embraced the formalists' view in his confirmation hearings before the United States Senate by asserting that he saw his job as a judge as akin to that of an 'umpire' in baseball.[12] He might well have meant this to be an assertion that he disdains the idea of acting as a 'super legislator', but his analogy implicitly accepts the model of

7 *See* G. Keren & Y. Schul, 'Two Is Not Always Better Than One: A Critical Evaluation of Two-System Theories', *Perspectives on Psychological Science*, Vol. 4, No. 6, pp. 533-550.

8 *See* Kahneman 2011.

9 *See* Guthrie *et al.* 2007.

10 *See* J.C. Hutcheson, Jr., 'The Judgment Intuitive: The Function of the "Hunch" in Judicial Decision', *Cornell Law Quarterly* 1929, Vol. 14, No. 2, pp. 285-288.

11 *See* B. Neuborne, 'Of Sausage Factories and Syllogism Machines: Formalism, Realism, and Exclusionary Selection Techniques', *New York University Law Review* 1992, Vol. 67, No. 2, pp. 419-449.

12 *See* M.N. Berman, 'Constitutional Interpretation: Non-Originalism', *Philosophical Compass* 2011, Vol. 6, No. 6, pp. 408-420.

judges as syllogistic machines. Commentators in the academy asserted that Justice Roberts' statement was overly simplistic and presents a view of judging that is too mechanical.[13] Judging is surely not as mechanistic as that metaphor suggests. Rules and precedent are too fuzzy and malleable to allow judges to restrict their efforts to calling balls and strikes. Chief Justice Roberts' comments in a highly visible public forum, however, suggest that a great many people believe that judges should aspire to a highly mechanical approach. The desire to have judges behave as umpires implies that judges should rely entirely on system 2 to make judgment.

The psychological research that supports the dual-process model, however, rejects the thesis that judges should ignore system 1. As practical matter, this would be impossible. System 1 operates in a largely automatic, almost effortless fashion.[14] Even outside of the courtroom, most choices almost instantly produce a hunch or an intuition as to the ultimate preference, even before people think things through fully. This initial impression can then guide (or misguide) the deliberative system, thus making it nearly impossible to avoid the influence of intuitive judgment.

Beyond the practical difficulties of ignoring one's intuition, it would be unwise to do so completely. In studies of individuals who lack strong intuitive systems, neuroscientist Anthony Damasio demonstrates why this would be a problem.[15] Such individuals must rely entirely on their deliberative systems to make judgments. If judging is like umpiring, then these people should make great judges. But in fact, they are terrible decision makers. Although they can articulate the pros and cons of almost any choice with great acumen, these pros and cons seem to move them not at all to make a choice. Decision making seems to require an emotional component in order to create the confidence needed to make a final commitment to one choice or another. A non-intuitive judge would thus likely lack the confidence and fortitude needed to make the difficult choices that come before judges. The idea that judges should act as umpires is compelling, but it is likely misleading.

The psychological research suggests that neither the formalist nor the realist position can be completely accurate. Outside of the courtroom people rely on both systems of reasoning to make judgments. Judges, too, likely need both systems of reasoning to make choices. Although the idea that judges should be umpires is not entirely correct, the metaphor has some bite for an important reason that the psychological research suggests. That is, the two systems of reasoning are not entirely in balance. System 1 produces fast, confident judgments in an effortless fashion. Indeed, this is

---

13 *See id.*

14 *See* Kahneman 2011.

15 A.R. Damasio, *Descartes' Error: Emotion, Reason, and the Human Brain*, New York: Putnam 1994.

the reason that psychologists call the intuitive system 'system 1'. System 1 allows us to react quickly in an emergency. Human ancestors who spotted a tiger approaching, would be well advised to run without thinking carefully about which way to run or whether the flight would be worth the effort. Any human that failed to make the quick judgment to flee in the face of danger, and instead calculated carefully the costs and benefits of doing so would be quickly eliminated from the gene pool. But system 1 can lead to predictable mistakes, and accurate judgment thus requires engaging in some cognitive effort to check one's intuitions against logic.

The model of good judging that I advance here does not suggest entirely rejecting system 1 reasoning. Rather, I suggest that judges follow the model used by chess grandmasters when playing tournaments.[16] Not surprisingly, chess grandmasters have a set of well-developed intuitions about chess. When presented with a chess board, they will instantly have an intuition about an appropriate next move – and it will be a good move. This ability enables chess grandmasters to beat most players at 'lightening chess', and to play dozens of games against multiple players all at once. But then why do matches between grandmasters typically take hours? Intuition, after all, produces rapid judgments. In fact, in tournaments grandmasters check their intuitions about moves carefully, slowly, and deliberatively. Chess grandmasters will replace their intuitive move with one that they derive through intuition roughly half of the time. Understanding when to replace intuition is the key to sound judgment and understanding how people decide when to replace their intuitive judgments is also therefore the key to knowing how good judgments are made.

Good judgment in many contexts, including in the courtroom, follows a similar pattern of intuition that is sometimes overridden with deliberation. Judges need intuition to drive the decision making process, just as we all do. But to ensure that they are making accurate decisions, judges must also check their intuition with careful, deliberative processes. Most people make most important judgments in most contexts in this manner. Although it does not seem likely that judges are any different, it is possible that they are. Legal reasoning has strong deductive, rule-oriented components. As such, the profession of judging might attract people who are more prone to rely on deliberative reasoning. Alternatively, training and experience as a judge might teach judges to distrust intuition and rely on deliberation. Some professionals, such as engineers or mathematicians, seem more naturally prone to deliberative thinking than others. Perhaps judges are similar.

To assess judges' deliberative and intuitive tendencies, my collaborators, Chris Guthrie and Andrew Wistrich, and I have gathered data on several thousand trial

16 *See* T. Mueller, 'Your Move', *The New Yorker*, 12 December 2005, pp. 62.

judges in the United States and Canada over the past twelve years. We have described our methods in detail elsewhere.[17] Briefly put, we attend judicial education conferences at which we administer brief questionnaires containing hypothetical scenarios that request legal judgments. In some cases we present judges with logical problems without any legal context. We design the hypothetical questions and logical problems to assess whether judges tend to rely on the same kinds of cognitive processes as ordinary adults.

Although most of our questions involve legal scenarios, we have presented logical problems to judges to assess their general propensity to rely too heavily on intuition. We have presented a common test of reasoning known as the 'cognitive reflection test' ('CRT') to several groups of judges. The CRT is a simple, three-item test developed by Shane Frederick to assess people's propensities to rely too heavily on intuition.[18] The CRT consists of three items:

(1) A bat and a ball cost $1.10 in total. The bat costs $1.00 more than the ball. How much does the ball cost? _____cents

(2) If it takes 5 machines 5 minutes to make 5 widgets, how long would it take 100 machines to make 100 widgets? _____minutes

(3) In a lake, there is a patch of lily pads. Every day, the patch doubles in size. If it takes 48 days for the patch to cover the entire lake, how long would it take for the patch to cover half of the lake? _____days

Each of the three CRT items has a correct answer that is easy to understand, but each also has an intuitive, but incorrect, answer that almost immediately comes to mind to most people.[19] Most people think that 10 cents is the correct answer to the first problem. Though intuitive, this answer is wrong, as a bit of reflection shows. If the ball costs 10 cents, and the bat costs one dollar more, this means that the bat costs $1.10. Adding those two figures together, the total cost of the bat and ball would be $1.20, not $1.10, as specified by the problem. The correct answer is thus five cents. That is, the ball costs five cents, the bat costs $1.05, and together, they cost $1.10. Similarly, most people respond to the implicit numeric alliteration of the second question with the answer of 100. This answer is also wrong because if five machines make five widgets in five minutes, this means that each machine makes one widget in that five-minute time period. Thus, it would take only five minutes for 100 machines to produce 100 widgets (just like 200 machines would make 200 widgets in that same

17 Guthrie *et al.* 2001; Guthrie *et al.* 2007; A.J. Wistrich, C. Guthrie & J.J. Rachlinski, 'Can Judges Ignore Inadmissible Information: The Difficulty of Deliberately Disregarding', *University of Pennsylvania Law Review* 2004, Vol. 153, No. 4, pp. 1253-1345.

18 S. Frederick, 'Cognitive Reflection and Decision Making', *Journal of Economic Perspectives* 2005, Vol. 19, No. 4, pp. 25-42.

19 *Id.*

five-minute period). The third question combines the 'one half' with the 48 to make it seem like 24 is the right answer, but this is also wrong. The correct answer, obvious upon reflection, is 47 days. If the patch of lily pads doubles each day and fully covers the lake on the 48th day, it will cover half the lake the day before. Thus, the correct answer is 47 days, not 24 days.

The CRT items are simple in that 'their solution is easily understood when explained', but 'reaching the correct answer often requires the suppression of an erroneous answer that springs "impulsively" to mind'.[20] Most people are unable or unwilling to suppress that impulsive response, however. In 35 separate studies involving 3,428 respondents, Frederick found that subjects, on average, got 1.24 of the three items correct, though responses varied across the subject pools.[21] For example, students at the University of Toledo obtained an average score of 0.57, while students at Massachusetts Institute of Technology obtained an average score of 2.18. Among all of the subjects tested, only 17% got all three questions correct; nearly twice that many (33%) got all three questions wrong.

The CRT illustrates the operation of two systems of reasoning in three respects. First, people perform poorly on the CRT, even though the questions are easy. The problems are not like those on a test of intelligence, which tax the deliberative system's abilities. Rather, they test the willingness to engage the deliberative system. Second, the intuitive answers identified above (10 cents in the bat-and-ball problem, 100 minutes in the widget problem, and 24 days in the lily-pad problem) are the most common wrong answers provided. This shows that the source of the wrong answers lies with the reliance on the intuitive system. Third, people who select the intuitive answers believe that the problems are easier than those who answer correctly. In the bat-and-ball problem, for instance, subjects who provided the intuitive response (10 cents) predicted that 92% of people would solve the problem correctly. By contrast, subjects who responded correctly predicted that only 62% of people would do so.[22] The intuitive system produces highly confident judgments, and hence those who rely on intuitive judgment are more confident.

If judges are, by nature, deliberative individuals, they should perform much more like Massachusetts Institute of Technology undergraduates on the CRT than like ordinary adults. To test this, we presented the CRT to a group of nearly 300 trial judge as in attendance at a judicial conference in Florida.[23] Our results largely track those

20 *Id.*, p. 27.
21 *Id.*
22 *Id.*
23 Guthrie *et al.* 2007, p. 4.

of ordinary adults, and not MIT students. Most of the judges got most of the question wrong. They scored an average of 1.23 out of three correct. Comparing this result to others, they are not as quite as deliberative as Harvard Undergraduates (who averaged 1.42 correct), but score higher than adult subjects obtained from an internet sample (who averaged 1.10 correct). As with other groups, the most commonly chosen wrong answers were the intuitive ones: 97%, 60%, and 58% chose the intuitive answer for each question, respectively. Furthermore, we also asked these judges what percentage of judges in the room would get each question correct and, like other groups, those who chose the intuitive answer thought the questions were easier than those who chose the right answer. On the first question, for example, judges who chose the intuitive answer asserted that, on average, 90% of the judges would get the question right, as opposed to an average of 66% among those who got the question right.

Although these results show judges to rely too heavily intuition in decision making, the problems are not set in a legal context. Most of our research program, however, illustrates how judges rely too extensively on their intuition while making judgments in legal settings. We have found that judges are excellent decision makers on the whole. They resist the pull of intuition in some surprising settings. In particular, we have found four general types of instances in which judges have difficulty suppressing their intuition: they attend to cues that lead them to focus on irrelevant aspects of a case; they rely on misleading numeric reference points; they try to make judgments that are consistent with their emotional reactions to litigants; and they seem to suffer from confirmation bias.

5.1 Context and Format Effects

Intuition can be manipulated by simple contextual cues. Seemingly irrelevant aspects of a decision making problem can direct a decision maker's attention to different aspects of a multi-faceted problem. The research of psychologist Seymor Epstein provides a useful example of how context can trigger misleading intuition. In one of his studies, he and his co-author gave participants an opportunity to win $20 if they could draw a red jellybean from an urn filled with red and white jellybeans while blindfolded.[24] Epstein gave the participants a choice of drawing from an urn filled with 1 red and 9 white jellybeans or an urn filled with 10 red and 90 white jellybeans. Even though the chances of success are identical, most participants chose to draw from the urn with the larger number of balls. Epstein contends that the intuitive system induces people to see more chances to win in the large urn, while blinding them

24 L.A. Kirkpatrick & S. Epstein, 'Cognitive-Experiential Self-Theory and Subjective Probability: Further Evidence for Two Conceptual Systems', *Journal of Personality and Social Psychology* 1992, Vol. 63, No. 4, pp. 534-544.

to the fact that there are also more chances to lose. People must use basic mathematics with their deliberative system to see the urns as identical. Making matters worse, people seem to prefer the larger urn, even if there are fewer than ten red jellybeans in the large urn. Even when only seven red jellybeans are present in the larger urn, fully half of the participants chose the smaller urn. Just as those who choose the wrong answers on the CRT fail to override their intuition, so too do Epstein's subjects unwisely rely solely on their intuition.

Epstein's 'jellybean phenomenon' translates directly into an important legal context – that of involuntary civil commitment. In most jurisdictions in the United States, mentally disturbed individuals may be confined against their will if a judge determines that they pose a danger to themselves or to others. This determination is almost invariably aided by expert testimony from mental health professionals. As the science of assessing the dangerousness of mentally disturbed individuals has become more precise, such testimony increasingly produces specific probability estimates of the likelihood that such individuals will commit violent acts. Presumably, the greater the likelihood of violence, the greater will be the justification for an involuntary commitment.

Although the risk of violence should affect civil commitment decisions, the format in which a clinician communicates that risk should not. Epstein's jellybean phenomena suggests, however, that telling a judge that 1 out of 10 individuals will commit a violent act will have a different effect than telling a judge that 10 out of 100 individuals will commit a violent act. Researchers have demonstrated that this exact variation influences clinicians' judgments. [25] If even experts are subject to this effect, then it seems unlikely that judges will be able to resist it.

Monahan and Silver, in fact, have demonstrated that judges seem vulnerable to the kind misleading intuitive phenomena that Epstein suggests.[26] They gave trial judges from across the United States attending a judicial education conference a hypothetical case of a mentally disturbed individual to evaluate for civil commitment. They then asked the judges to identify the threshold probability of violence that they felt would be necessary to justify a civil commitment. For half of the judges, they offered five choices: 1%, 8%, 26%, 56%, and 75%. For the other half, they offered the same choices, but presented them in a frequency format. That is, the judges in this version chose between the following options: 1 in 100, 8 in 100, 26 in 100, 56 in 100, and 75 in

25 P. Slovic, J. Monahan & D. MacGregor, 'Violence Risk Assessment and Risk Communication: The Effect of Using Actual Cues, Providing Instruction, and Employing Probability Versus Frequency Formats', *Law and Human Behavior* 2000, Vol. 24, No. 3, pp. 271-96.

26 J. Monahan & E. Silver, 'Judicial Decision Thresholds for Violence Risk Management', *International Journal of Forensic Mental Health* 2003, Vol. 2, No. 1, pp. 1-6.

100. The probabilities in all five offered choices were identical, but the variation produced a reaction. Judges who assessed percentages selected a modal threshold of 26%, but judges who assessed frequencies selected a threshold of 8 in 100. Monahan and Silver reasoned that the frequency format produced the same kind of focus on the numerator that affected Epstein's subjects. Specifically, the '8 in 100' choice implies that 8 people might be at risk from a decision not to inter the individual. Alternatively, the frequency format made it clear to judges that if made such decision on a regular basis, a fairly large number of people might become victims of violence.

In our own work, we have shown similar influences that the scale or the format has on judges' judgment. We asked a group of judges attending a national educational conference in the United States to sentence a hypothetical criminal defendant. In all cases, the defendant had been convicted of voluntary manslaughter. The materials for the hypothetical indicated that the victim had taunted the defendant while the two were together in a bar, claiming to have had intercourse with his fiancé. The materials also described the defendant as having one prior arrest, but lacking any significant criminal past. The defendant became enraged and stabbed the victim with a steak knife. We asked the judges, 'regardless of the sentencing system in your home jurisdiction, what sentence do you think is appropriate for this defendant'. The materials then provided a blank space for the judges in which to provide a sentence. For half of the judges, this blank was followed by the word 'years' and for the other half, it was followed by the word 'months'. In effect, we asked judges to sentence the defendant on one of two different scales – months or years.

The scale had a profound effect on the judges. The judges who sentenced in years imposed an average sentence of 9.6 years, while the judges who sentenced in months imposed an average sentence of 67 months – which corresponds to only 5.6 years. In the United States, some states (and the federal criminal system) administer sentences in months, while others dole out punishment in years. Our national sample of judges, therefore, included judges who had to identify a sentence using an unfamiliar scale. Judges who normally sentence in years might have had have difficulty using months and vice versa. The deviations that such unfamiliarity might have produced, however, had a systematic effect. Judges were unwilling to increase their sentences to match the appropriately large number of months. The scale thus had an enormous effect on judgment.

In these studies, background characteristics that are irrelevant to the underlying decision, such as whether expert testimony is offered in probability of frequency format or whether the scale of sentences is years or months, had a profound effects on judge's judgment. In Monahan and Silver's study, eight in a hundred felt more dangerous to judges than did an eight per cent risk of violence. Likewise, even though 9.6 years seemed like a fair sentence to judges assessing in years, apparently the equivalent in months (115) seemed too lengthy a sentence to the judges. The format and scale created intuitions that changed how judges thought about these cases.

5.2 Anchoring

The evidence that background context can produce different intuitions that lead to different judicial decisions also suggests that a phenomenon known as anchoring can also influence judge's judgment. Anchoring is the tendency to rely on numeric reference points to make numeric judgments.[27] This tendency is often reasonable, as numeric reference points commonly provide useful information as to the appropriate judgment. For example, the list price of an automobile or a house is apt to give the potential buyer a good deal of information as to how much they will ultimately pay for the commodity, once negotiation is complete. Decades of research, however, reveal that numeric reference points influence judgment, even when they obviously convey no information.[28] Even ludicrous anchors influence people's judgment. In one demonstration of this, undergraduates were asked to identify the average price of a textbook in the bookstore. Half of these subjects were first asked whether the average price was greater or less than $7,128.53.[29] Those who were given the absurdly high anchor gave higher estimates than those who were not. In another demonstration, researchers had undergraduates guess the year in which Attila the Hun was defeated in Europe by writing down the last three digits of their phone number, adding 400 to the result, placing the letters 'A.D.' after the result, and then first guessing whether the year was before or after the result.[30] Even though the anchor is transparently unrelated to the event, subjects' estimates still correlated with their phone numbers.

Anchoring potentially poses a serious concern for judges. When imposing criminal sentences and identifying civil damage awards, judges must make numerical estimates reliably, even though they might be exposed to a wide range of potentially misleading anchors. Both kinds of judgments are extremely difficult to make reliably. A reliable criminal sentence must incorporate a wide range of factors, including the defendant's personal history, criminal record, and nature of the offense, into a single numeric assessment. Civil damages require translating a qualitative assessment of life and limb into a monetary amount. Furthermore, a series of mock jury studies show that litigants requests for particular damage awards can have profound effects

27 *See* Tversky & Kahneman 1974.

28 *See* D. Ariel, *Predictably Irrational: The Hidden Forces That Shape Our Decisions, Revised & Expanded Edition*, New York: Harper Perennial 2010.

29 Reported in S. Plous, *The Psychology of Judgment and Decision Making*, New York: McGraw-Hill 1993, pp. 146.

30 J.E. Russo & P.J.H. Schoemaker, *Decision Traps: The Ten Barriers to Decision Making and How to Overcome Them*, New York: Simon & Schuster 1990.

on damage awards, even when these requests are ludicrous.[31] These factors suggest that numeric requests from litigants, irrelevant information about a case, or even numeric amounts involving other cases might affect judges.

We have conducted several demonstrations of the effects of numeric anchors on judges. In one study,[32] we asked administrative law judges in the United States to identify an appropriate damage award for a hypothetical civil rights violation filed with a city human rights commission. We gave the judges a full page of details about the case. The case involved an administrative assistant named 'Veronica', who worked for a firm that did contract work for a major city. The materials indicated that Veronica had a good employment record, but that a new manager began calling her racially derogatory names and insulting her nationality (the materials stated that she was Mexican American) in front of friends and co-workers. When she complained, he fired her. The materials then stated that Veronica obtained another position right away, which meant that damages arising from her complaint were limited to 'mental anguish'.

The materials describe some measure of suffering arising from the incident, and include some testimony by Veronica. In one version of the testimony, Veronica asserts that she recently saw a case similar to hers on a 'court television show where the plaintiff received a compensatory damage award for mental anguish'. In the other version, we added the number $415,300 before the word 'compensatory'. In all cases, the testimony is irrelevant and inadmissible. But the variation exposed half of the judges to a high anchor. Just as happened with undergraduates given an arbitrarily high anchor for the average price of textbooks, judges exposed to the high anchor in our study gave much higher estimates of damage awards. Judges exposed to the anchor gave a median award of $50,000 while those not exposed gave a median award of only $6,250.

We have also found that anchoring affects sentencing decisions. In a study involving a group of newly appointed trial judges, we asked the judges to sentence two different criminal defendants, who had been found guilty of unrelated crimes. One of the defendants was found guilty of assault with a deadly weapon. The materials described this defendant as having threatened a colleague with an unloaded handgun as part of an argument involving a debt that the victim supposedly owed to the defendant. The materials (accurately) indicated that the maximum sentence for this crime was

31 G.B. Chapman & B.H. Bornstein, 'The More You Ask For the More You Get: Anchoring in Personal Injury Verdicts', *Applied Cognitive Psychology* 1996, Vol. 10, No. 6, pp. 519-540.

32 C. Guthrie, J.J. Rachlinski & A.J. Wistrich, 'The "Hidden Judiciary": An Empirical Examination of Executive Branch Justice', *Duke Law Journal* 2009, Vol. 58, No. 7, pp. 1477-1530.

three years imprisonment. The other defendant was found guilty of voluntary manslaughter. The materials described this defendant as having had stabbed a victim to death in a bar after the victim taunted him about a sexual encounter with his fiancé. The materials (accurately) indicated that the maximum sentence for this crime was fifteen years. The materials clearly stated that these two crimes were unrelated. Half of the judges first read about the defendant convicted of assault, followed by the manslaughter, whereas the other half of the judges read the cases in the opposite order.

The order in which the defendants were sentence should not have affected their sentences. The crimes were unrelated and even if they were related, the judges should have been able to weigh the severity of the crime and the circumstances of the defendant independently. And yet, order mattered. Judges who sentenced the manslaughter first assigned this defendant an average of 8.6 years, whereas judges who sentenced the manslaughter after the assault only assigned an average of 6.1 years. Contemplating the lesser sentenced made a lengthy sentence seem less appropriate to the judges. Judges who sentenced the assault first assigned an average of 1.2 years, whereas judges who sentenced the assault after the manslaughter assigned an average of 1.6 years. Contemplating the lengthy prison sentence for the manslaughter made a short sentence for the assault seem too short. The unrelated sentencing decision provided an anchor for the judges that influenced their assessment of the appropriate prison sentence.

We have also found that anchors influenced judges in several other contexts. Notably, reminding federal judges in the United States of the jurisdictional minimum amount for certain types of civil cases in the federal courts ($75,000) reduced otherwise large damage awards.[33] This jurisdictional minimum was well known to the judges and reminding them of the amount conveyed no information to the judges about the case at hand. Nevertheless, the reminder affected their awards. Similarly, in another study, disclosing settlement offers to judges influenced the damage awards they assigned, even when the materials reminded judges that such offers are not admissible.[34]

Judges react differently to cases when they face numeric reference points, almost without regard for the source of those reference points. These reference points act as anchors that influence how judges process cases.

33 Guthrie *et al.* 2001.
34 Wistrich *et al.* 2004.

5.3. Consistency Seeking

System 1 prefers simplicity. Intuition often arises from close associations, so for the intuitive brain, like goes with like. The intuitive brain prefers that likeable litigants win their cases. Litigants who have positive attributes should thus capture the intuitive brain's attention and facilitate legal rulings that are consistent with the impression that a litigant makes. As Clarence Darrow put it:

> 'Jurymen seldom convict a person they like, or acquit one they dislike. The main work of the trial lawyer is to make a jury like his client, or at least to feel sympathy for him.'[35]

Ignoring irrelevant attributes that make a litigant seem favourable or unfavourable requires the deliberative mind. The intuitive mind likes a consistent, simple picture in which good people win their cases and bad people lose.

Several types of studies demonstrate the role that efforts to maintain consistency play in legal judgments. For example, mock jury studies suggest that attractive criminal defendants are less likely to be found guilty than less attractive criminal defendants, and draw shorter sentences.[36] Psychologists have long written about the effects of attractiveness as form of consistency called a 'halo effect'. That is, the intuitive brain treats people with a positive appearance as if they are also apt to have a positive personality.

Professor Dan Simon has conducted a series of studies showing the importance of consistency in legal judgments.[37] He has shown that adults will try to ensure that their assessments of legal principles conform to their views about the litigants themselves, even though the litigants' attributes are irrelevant. Litigants who are likeable induce people to make assessments of abstract legal problems that are favourable to their litigation positions, even when a litigant's likability is irrelevant to the legal judgment.

We have found similar results in trial judges. In a study of both state and federal judges, we asked judges to make a judgment about law that is unrelated to the characteristics of the defendant while varying the defendant's characteristics. We described an illegal immigrant who was being held for entering the United States with a forged

35 E.H. Sutherland & D.R. Cressey, *Principles of Criminology*, (7th edn.), Lanham, MD: AltaMira Press 1966, p. 442.

36 V.P. Hans & N. Vidmar, *Judging the Jury*, Cambridge, MA: Perseus Publishing 1986, p. 133.

37 D. Simon, 'A Third View of the Black Box: Cognitive Coherence in Legal Decision Making', *University of Chicago Law Review* 2004, Vol. 71, No. 3, pp. 511-586.

visa. The defendant had obtained a fake visa, which he had pasted into a genuine Peruvian passport. The materials indicated that possession and use of the fake visa obviously subjected the defendant to arrest and deportation, but a further question remained. The prosecutor had also charged the defendant with forging an identification document – namely his passport. Although the passport was genuine, the question of whether pasting a false document on it constituted forgery of the underlying passport remained. We provided the text of relevant statutes, which did not clearly determine the matter. Our materials also informed the judges that no precedent could be found on the subject. The materials indicated that if pasting the fake visa on the genuine passport constituted forgery of an identification document, then the defendant would spend extra time in prison before being deported, whereas if it did not, then he would simply be deported. For half of the judges, the materials described the immigrant as having entered the United States to earn extra money to pay for an operation for his sick nine-year-old daughter; for the other half, the materials indicate that the immigrant had entered the United States to track down a rogue member of a drug cartel.

The legal ruling that our materials required judges to make was unrelated to the background of the defendant. The underlying legal judgment was a difficult one, but the reasons that the defendant entered the United States were not relevant to the decision. Nevertheless, the reasons affected the judges. When the materials identified the defendant as a sympathetic father, only 40% ruled that he had committed forgery. When the materials identified the defendant as a potential assassin, however, 60% of the judges ruled that he had committed forgery. Just as ordinary adults in Simon's work tried to make their legal judgments correspond to their views of the litigants, judges in our study tended to conform their legal ruling to their reaction to the defendant's character.

Intuition thus seems to be at work in judgments about legal rulings that would otherwise seem unrelated to the facts. To be sure, sympathy was not wholly dispositive. In our results, the sympathetic father still lost 40% of the time, and the unsavory drug dealer still won 40% of the time. But litigant's irrelevant background influenced judge's rulings on legal issues, suggesting that intuition plays an important role in how judges reason about law. The influence of intuition can be benign or even helpful if a litigant's characteristics are related to the judge's ruling. For example, in our study, we also asked judges to sentence the defendant, and the assassin drew appropriately higher sentences than the father. But when the judges are making legal rulings that create precedent for future cases, which might have different facts, they need to be more careful not to let irrelevant features of a case interfere with their judgment.

One interesting aspect of this problem we discovered was that new judges seemed less influenced by intuition than more seasoned judges. We attempted to replicate this study on a group of new trial judges and found that roughly 70% of the judges ruled against the immigrant, regardless of whether he was identified as an assassin or a father. This result demonstrates two interesting aspects. First, new judges did a better job of ignoring irrelevant influences than senior judges. Second, the results suggest that some of the more seasoned judges were altering their rulings to reflect sympathy for the father (rather than altering their rulings as a way of further to punishing the assassin). In effect, the new judges declined to act on the sympathy that the father evoked. This difference might reflect a greater degree of confidence among the senior judges that they should follow their intuition, and allow their sympathies to affect how they rule on matters of law.

The role of intuition and emotion in cases like ours might be more normatively ambiguous than the role intuition plays in other contexts. It might be appropriate for seasoned judges to place some faith in their sympathies. Perhaps judges can and should bend the law little to do some justice in an individual case, without fear that they are creating undesirable precedent. Experienced judges might be more inclined to think that future cases with less sympathetic litigants can perhaps be distinguished. Judges who are new to the role, in contrast, are more worried about letting their sympathies influence how they rule on matters of law.

5.4 Confirmation Bias

Not only does the intuitive preference for consistency affect how people judge facts, it also affects what kinds of evidence people examine. For nearly fifty years, psychologists have documented evidence that people suffer from a confirmation bias in assessing their beliefs.[38] This bias refers to the tendency to search for evidence that can confirm an existing belief, while ignoring evidence that might disconfirm an existing belief. So potent is this bias that people will look for confirmation of their beliefs among irrelevant sources of evidence before they look for sources that might undermine their beliefs.

The clearest demonstration of the bias is the Wason card-selection task, first discussed nearly fifty years ago.[39] In this experiment, participants face four cards, and are told that each of them has a letter on one side and a number on the other. The cards read as follows: E, P, 4, and 7. The participants are then asked to test the hypothesis that 'if there is a vowel on one side of the card, then there is an even number on the other

38 *See* R.J. MacCoun, 'Biases in the Interpretation and Use of Research Results', *Annual Review of Psychology* 1998, Vol. 49, No.1, pp. 259-287.

39 P.C. Wason, 'Reasoning', *in*: B.M. Foss (Ed.), *New Horizons in Psychology*, Harmondsworth: Penguin 1966, pp. 131-151.

side'. They are then asked to turn over those cards – and only those cards – that are required to test this hypothesis. Only two cards actually provide any evidence on the hypothesis. Most participants correctly turn over the card showing the letter 'E', but then typically turn over the card showing a '4', or all of the cards. Turning over all of the cards disregards the instructions, which indicate that the participants should use as few cards as possible. The card showing the 'P' is transparently irrelevant, as the hypothesis does not make any claims regarding what might be on the other side of consonants. But the card showing a '4' is also irrelevant. Finding a vowel on the other side of this card would seem to confirm the hypothesis, but the consonant would not undermine the hypothesis, which makes no claim about what lies on the other side of consonants. Because the '4' card cannot either confirm or disconfirm the hypothesis, there is no need to turn it over. The card showing a '7', however, is important. If a vowel lurks on the other side of this card, then the hypothesis is false. Thus, the 'E' and the '7' are the correct answer, although typically fewer than 10% of the participants choose only these two cards.

Psychologists have interpreted the results of the Wason task to support the idea that people engage in motivated searches for evidence supporting their beliefs.[40] Even in this abstract setting, people fail to appreciate the importance of investigating the possibility that their theories are wrong. Numerous studies of motivated reasoning and inference suggest that this problem is even more severe when the beliefs are important.[41] People engage in a kind of wishful thinking that leads them to avoid looking for evidence that might suggest that their beliefs are mistaken and to avoid searching for any kind of disconfirming evidence.

Confirmation bias can create serious problems within the legal system. A factfinder suffering from the influence of the confirmation bias will allow an initial theory to influence how they gather and process subsequent information. In effect, the first impression might be the last. An adversarial process might combat the influence of the bias by allowing parties to expose the factfinder to disconfirming evidence. Factfinders might discount evidence that disconfirms their initial biases, but a convincing presentation might shake a factfinder's initial beliefs. The confirmation bias likely poses the greatest risk to prosecutors and judges in inquisitorial systems because initial beliefs will guide further inquiry. A prosecutor or judge might fail to consider looking for the kind of information that would undermine their initial belief that a particular suspect is guilty. Several studies in which subjects asked to act as prosecutors in reviewing a case file demonstrate that people avoid looking for disconfirming

40 *See* MacCoun 1998.
41 *Ibid.*

evidence and discount the importance of such evidence when they encounter it, even in legal settings.[42]

Trial judges also suffer from confirmation bias. In one study, we gave trial judges the original version of the Wason card-selection task, as described above. Only 9% got the problem right. As with other groups, most judges indicated that they would need to turn over the even-numbered card to test the hypothesis that the cards containing vowels on one side have even numbers on the other. Other judges indicated that they would need to overturn all four cards. As with our results on the CRT, these results suggest that judges do not suppress their intuition on abstract problems.

As with other reasoning problems we have investigated, we are more concerned with problems that have realistic content. For the confirmation bias, realistic content is particularly important, because in some settings, researchers have found that contextual cues can lead people to identify the correct solution. For example, Cosmides and Tooby found that when people are applying well-understood social rules, such as 'only people over the age of 21 may drink alcohol', they target their inquiries carefully.[43] In this particular example, researchers asked people to ascertain whether a bar is enforcing the drinking age by investigating four people: a person who is drinking beer, a person who is drinking a soft drink, a person who is under 21, and a person who is over 21. People tended to identify the correct targets needed to test the rule, which are the person drinking beer (who must be over 21) and the person who is under 21 (who must be drinking a soft drink). Imposing the context of a social rule on the materials invokes a familiar, understandable script that then makes the problem easy to solve. Judges might be particularly well-attuned to understanding rules like this. Hence, the abstract problem might not be a fair test for determining whether judges suffer from the confirmation bias in a more realistic setting.

To test the theory that rules and context helps judges avoid the confirmation bias, we added a legal context to the Wason task and presented it to trial judges. In fact, half of the judges evaluated only the barebones Wason problem while the other half evaluated a version that invoked anti-discrimination laws. In this version, we asked the judges to imagine that they were presiding over a gender discrimination complaint. The plaintiff had alleged that she was denied a promotion due to pervasive discrimination within her company. In this version, instead of stating the target hypothesis

42 E. Rassin, A. Eerland & I. Kuijpers, 'Let's Find the Evidence: An Analogue Study of Confirmation Bias in Criminal Investigations', *Journal of Investigative Psychology and Offender Profiling* 2010, Vol. 7, No. 3, pp. 231-246.

43 Leda Cosmides & John Tooby, 'Cognitive Adaptations for Social Exchange', *in*: J.H. Barkow, L. Cosmides & J. Tooby (Eds.), *The Adapted Mind: Evolutionary Psychology and the Generation of Culture*, New York: Oxford University Press 1992, pp 163-228.

that 'if there is a vowel on one side of the card, then there is an even number on the other side', we asked the judges to assess the allegation that 'male supervisors only promote male employees'. We informed the judges that the plaintiff had partial information on four instances of promotions within the company: a male supervisor who promoted an employee of unknown gender; a female supervisor who promoted an employee of unknown gender, a male employee who was recently promoted; and a female employee who was recently promoted. The materials then informed the judge that the unidentified gender in each of these decisions could only be obtained through further litigation. Although the materials indicated that the judges could order that these identities be uncovered, doing so would be expensive, and so they should only issue the order if the identifies were relevant. Because further effort would be expensive, we asked the judges to identify only those inquiries that would be necessary to test the hypothesis. The logical structure of the problem is identical to the Wason card selection task, with 'supervisors' substituted for 'letters' (with 'male' as 'vowel' and 'female' as 'consonant'), 'employees' substituted for 'numbers' (with 'male' as 'even' and female as 'odd'). If context facilitated correct responses, this familiar context should have helped judges identify the correct response.

In our study, context was little help to the judges. Only 14% identified the correct answer – only a modest improvement over the 9% accuracy rate we observed with the abstract materials. As with the original version of the problem, most of the judges recognized that they needed to investigate the decision made by a male supervisor; if he had promoted a female employee, the theory would be wrong, just as finding an odd number on the other side of the vowel would prove the theory wrong in the original version of the problem. Judges also tended to seek the gender of the person who promoted the male employee, just as they tended to think that the letter on the other side of the odd number was important. Several of the judges also incorrectly stated that all four decisions needed to be investigated, just as several in the original version indicated that all four cards needed to be turned over.

These results suggest that the confirmation bias might be an important influence on judges. Because we only investigated one example, this study cannot rule out the possibility that other kinds of contexts would facilitate more accurate responses from judges. But our results suggest that the training and experience that judges have, combined with a familiar legal context does not facilitate a deliberative, logical analysis of this kind of a problem.

5.5 Conclusion

Judges have a strong intuitive side. In several contexts, judges seem to prefer intuitive judgments, even though intuition leads them astray. This preference for intuition is evident most clearly on logical problems, like those in the CRT and in the Wason card selection task. Judges also seem to rely on their intuition in legal settings, however. In a series of studies, we have shown that judges rely on intuitive mental shortcuts that can lead them to make unreasonable judgments.

These results echo Jerome Frank's timeless observation that 'in the end, we must face the fact that judges are human'.[44] This observation has important descriptive and prescriptive components. Descriptively, judges are fallible in predictable ways, just as ordinary adults and other professionals are fallible. Prescriptively, this means any legal system must find ways to encourage judges to engage their deliberative faculties. Judges must stop and think to check their intuition against reality. Legal settings that facilitate this effort will likely encourage sound legal judgments, while those that encourage judges to rely on their intuition will be prone to error.

44 Frank 1949.

Contributors

Carsten K.W. de Dreu, professor of psychology, University of Amsterdam.

Raimond W.M. Giard, professor of tort law, Erasmus School of Law, Erasmus University Rotterdam and clinical pathologist Maasstad Ziekenhuis Rotterdam.

Ivo Giesen, professor of civil law and civil procedure, Utrecht University.

Jeffrey J. Rachlinski, professor of law, Cornell University Law School and Chair of Empirical Legal Studies at Erasmus School of Law, Erasmus University Rotterdam.

Femke S. ten Velde, department of psychology, University of Amsterdam.

Civilology | Civilologie

In de reeks **Civilology | Civilologie** staat de bestudering van het civiele recht centraal, niet vanuit zuiver juridisch perspectief maar met gebruikmaking van inzichten uit sociaalwetenschappelijke disciplines zoals economie, psychologie en sociologie. Die disciplines in onderlinge samenhang kunnen onze kennis vergroten van de gedragsassumpties waar het privaatrecht zich van bedient, de effecten die het privaatrecht heeft op het gedrag van individuen en organisaties en van de betekenis die deze assumpties en effecten hebben voor privaatrechtelijke beleidsvorming, regelstelling en -toepassing. De delen in de reeks **Civilology | Civilologie** beogen aldus een beter inzicht te geven in hoe privaatrecht écht werkt. De reeks staat onder redactie van Willem van Boom (EUR) en Ivo Giesen (UU).

In the **Civilology | Civilologie** series, the focus is on how private law works in real life. Rather than analysing private law from a strictly legal doctrinal perspective, this series encompasses the combined use of insights from social sciences – ranging from economics to psychology and sociology – in order to analyze the behavioural assumptions underlying private law, to understand the effects it has on individuals, organizations and businesses and to appreciate the impact of both assumptions and effects on policymakers, legislatures and courts. The **Civilology | Civilologie** series is edited by Willem van Boom (Erasmus Law School) and Ivo Giesen (Utrecht School of Law).

9 789490 947491